From Staff Nurse to Manager

To order additional copies, please contact us.
BookSurge, LLC
www.booksurge.com
1-866-308-6235
orders@booksurge.com

CHRISTIE OSUAGWU AND
GODWIN OSUAGWU
Cover Design by Nic The Artist

FROM STAFF NURSE TO MANAGER

A Guide to Successful Role
Transition

2006

From Staff Nurse to Manager

TABLE OF CONTENTS

ACKNOWLEDGMENT

We are immensely grateful to Rosaline A. Olade, R.N., Ph.D of the University of Nebraska and Paula Russell, Ph.D, formerly of Tyler Junior College, Tyler, Texas, for taking time to review the manuscript, and for their helpful suggestions.

Dedicated To Our Loving Children:
Ijeoma Chisom Osuagwu
Earl Chibueze Osuagwu
Uzondu Chinedum Osuagwu

In Many Ways They Are The Sources Of Our Drive, And
The Pride Of Our Lives.

Christie C. Osuagwu
Godwin U. Osuagwu

Tyler, Texas
November 2005

PREFACE

As the healthcare industry positions itself in today's competitive market place, the leaders of various health organizations must be prepared for the changes and challenges that lie ahead. Nurses in particular must be ready to assume positions of leadership in the management of their organizations in this dynamic environment. There is thus a "call to arms" to meet this challenge beyond the clinical preparation reminiscent of traditional nursing education.

This book is intended to be a handy practical guide for nurses aspiring to become managers; for those already in management/supervisory positions, it is an additional resource. As a *"How to"* book, it does not indulge in the extensive use of theoretical jargon common in formal management literature, neither is it intended to replace any management text. Nurses are encouraged to increase their knowledge by reading related literature and by attending workshops/seminars. They can also acquire business skills through continuing education by taking college level business courses.

CHAPTER 1
GETTING PREPARED

Nursing Education

Throughout its history, traditional nursing education has largely focused on the clinical, i.e. technical, aspects of providing care. Very little emphasis is placed on the business management component of nursing education. At best, most BSN programs offer one class in leadership while none is offered at the associate diploma level. Neither option effectively prepares professional nurses for the kind of challenges they would face in a managerial or supervisory position; thus some nurses who find themselves in such positions become easily overwhelmed and frustrated.

A number of things could be done to tackle this problem as far as it affects nurses. The nursing school curriculum, especially at the baccalaureate level, needs to include courses in business administration in order to strengthen the student's administrative skills and knowledge upon graduation. Graduate nursing programs should devote at least twenty-five percent of academic work to business management and technology courses, while the remaining seventy-five percent should be in the student's area of nursing concentration. Clinical internships during course work should be designed to include mandatory hours of actual managerial and supervisory exposure.

Other problems faced by nurses who aspire to management positions include the dearth of appropriate role models, the public's demeaning perception of the profession, and the way nurses are sometimes viewed by other health care professionals. Because nursing is also female dominated, it has not been viewed by society as a profession in its own right. Whatever their level of education and accomplishment, nurses are generally associated with *bedpans* and *custodial care,* hence some senior level administrators neither mentor nor empower nurses to take on administrative leadership roles. "It is sad that often those with neither the clinical training nor the appropriate business background make decisions that affect the life and career of not only nurses, but other members of the health care profession" (Osuagwu, 2004). This often leads to either a shallow appreciation of clinical matters or a one-dimensional perspective in the way healthcare organizations should be run. Hopefully, this posture will change as nursing becomes more recognized and respected as a profession in its own right, and as more men join the profession.

Nonetheless, slow progress is being made. Opportunities are beginning to present for specialization and upward mobility in the administrative ranks. Legislative initiatives brought about by health care reforms are affording nurses the opportunity to move away from the traditional hospital (inpatient) environment to rapidly expanding areas in either preventive, ambulatory, or home health services. Under the budget reconciliation bill passed by Congress at the end of July 1997, Nurse Practitioners and Clinical Nurse Specialists can now bill Medicare directly without physician supervision.

It is ironic that while these developments are good for the profession, most nurses still find themselves inadequately prepared for the leadership challenges in their new work roles.

Enhancing Personal and Professional Growth

If you dream of professional growth, aspire to obtain the BSN degree if you do not already have one. This is the basic academic qualification that is currently recognized for entry to the professional, *not vocational,* practice of Nursing. Nurses need to understand that preparation is the key to upward mobility. Once you are in practice, avail yourself of any opportunities to attend seminars and workshops on management development. Better still, you can embark on graduate work in either nursing, business administration or management, healthcare administration, public health, or any other field of your choice. You should not limit or short-change yourself by having a self-defeating attitude. Remember the age-old adage which still holds true: *knowledge is power.* It energizes.

A clinician who desires career advancement must become professionally active. You can accomplish this by belonging to a number of key professional associations as well as by offering to serve on various committees inside and outside your organization. Being professionally active enables you to keep up-to-date with changing trends, and affords you the privilege of belonging to a network of peers. Successful peers can inspire, challenge, support, and mentor you in your quest for self-improvement. They can also be points of contact for a career change at a later date. Subscribe to and read professional magazines, and attend job-related workshops, seminars, and conferences. At association meetings, make useful contributions; ask questions and learn the dynamics of working in a group.

When you return from professional meetings, seek out opportunities in your organization that will enable you apply some of what you have learned. Let your enthusiasm about a new process, procedure, or practice be *"infectious"* enough to attract your organization's interest – especially in specific terms such as cost-savings, revenue enhancement, process or methods improvement, and competitiveness. Arm yourself with knowledge and data, and be politically savvy in making any presentations. In a later section, we shall discuss organizational power and politics.

Many nurses tend to become so wrapped up with patient care that they pay less attention to self-improvement and to opportunities for administrative and supervisory growth. While you may not be in management now, you should be preparing and positioning yourself for the opportunity that may come. The future is for the visionary who is prepared and ready to capitalize on opportunities.

Make it a point to do a periodic self-assessment. This may reveal areas that need improvement such as:

- Interpersonal skills (including non-servile body language and self-confidence)
- Negotiating and conflict resolution skills, strategic positioning for personal and professional growth

- Communication skills (including what, when, where, how, and who to talk and listen to), and

- Dressing and personal aesthetics. Dress for the job you aspire to, not for the one you have now.

Environmental Changes

Management continues to evolve in response to the changes in the business and social environment. These changes are even more dramatic and competitive in the healthcare industry. They pose immense organizational challenges as well as require the application of business principles to the management and disbursement of healthcare dollars. During the mid to late 1980's, many hospitals unable to manage the concept of diagnosis related groups (DRGs) were forced out of the market. During the last few years, there has been a shift from hospital care to primary (ambulatory) care. Suddenly, all healthcare practitioners (nurses included) found themselves in the battle to efficiently manage their fiscal resources, and having to justify every single cent expended on healthcare delivery. Some healthcare institutions responded by outsourcing, establishing satellite clinics, developing PRN nurse pools, adopting managed care plans, embarking on improved billing techniques and applying other innovative management techniques such as cross-training in order to maximize human resources. Recent developments seem to indicate that these trends will continue.

The Future

What do these scenarios mean to the healthcare practitioner? They mean that nurse-managers, along with other healthcare providers, must become savvy in the management of resources and be proactive in planning for the future of healthcare delivery. A business leader in the New York-based Lee Hecht Harrison, an international career management firm, once stated that "the emerging healthcare workplace will allow healthcare professionals to function in a wider range of roles than ever before."[1]

As nurse-managers demonstrate competence in patient care, they also need to develop expertise in managing the material, financial, human, and other organizational resources under their control. Competitive positioning in the form of innovation, quality care to patients and sensitivity to their significant others, access, speed, vendor relationships, and employee needs will become critical. This fact takes on more significance in light of dwindling healthcare funding, managed competition, legal and regulatory changes/developments and human resource complexities. Other variables such as cost control, an increasingly diverse and demanding consumer population, and rapidly changing technology mandate increased knowledge as the staff nurse makes the transition to manager.

CHAPTER 2
MANAGEMENT BASICS

"The body of every organization is structured from four kinds of bones: WISHBONES spend all their time wishing someone else would do the work; JAWBONES do all the talking, but little else; KNUCKLEBONES knock everything anybody else tries to do; BACKBONES get under the load and do most of the work."

Author unknown

The question is which "bone" are you?

Managerial Misconceptions

Management is often misunderstood by many who aspire to it as a means of fulfilling a lifelong desire to attain power, influence, and control in organizations Nickels, McHugh and McHugh (2002) state that "organizations in the past were designed more to facilitate management than to please the customer." To others, management is something that should be dreaded and avoided by all means because it engenders an adversarial relationship between an organization and its workers or employees. Those who hold the latter view dread any semblance of confrontation, or are concerned with what we may refer to as the "Mosaic complex", i.e. a perceived sense of self-inadequacy. It is not uncommon for nurses to express their lack of desire for the *"headaches"* associated with being a manager or administrative leader. Many nurses prefer not to play the "dirty politics of management" and would rather put in *"my eight (clinical) hours and go home."* These expressions underscore a mental disposition toward leadership avoidance or management aversion often rooted in a deficiency in the various functional areas of planning, organizing, directing/leading, and controlling/evaluating. This deficiency is masked by a convenient avoidance of positions that call for administrative and decision-making responsibility. The opportunity to manage calls for a willingness to make a positive difference in one's organization by applying prudence in resource utilization, thus ensuring organizational prosperity, career growth and personal fulfillment.

Management Basics

Because of the nature of this book, this section will deal briefly with the very basics of management. In understanding these basics, however, it is necessary to first acquaint the nurse-manager with the various approaches to management. We will also explore the functions of management, types of managers, managerial roles, managerial skills, and leadership styles. Ivancevich et al (1997) synthesized the approaches to management into the classical approach, the behavioral approach, the decision and information sciences approach, the systems approach and the contingency approach.

A. *Classical Approach*

The classical approach is primarily concerned with increasing productivity by applying systematic methods aimed at improving efficiency in operations and control through prudent resource utilization and interdepartmental cooperation (Bateman and Snell, 2004). It consists of two distinct perspectives—*scientific management and administrative management.* Scientific management is centered on improving individual worker performance at the lower organizational level, and on identifying the "one best way" of doing a job. The earliest proponents of scientific management were Frederick W. Taylor (1856-1915) and Frank and Lilian Gilbreth (1868-1924 and 1878-1972 respectively). Administrative management emphasized the management of the total organization, focusing essentially on problems faced by top level managers. The earliest proponents of administrative management were Henri Fayol (1841-1925) and Max Weber (1864-1920). Weber's authority structures idealized efficient bureaucratic organizations through specialization of labor, authority, hierarchy, formal rules and procedures, and rigid promotion and selection criteria that ensured organizational impersonality. Fayol outlined the following fourteen principles of management:

1. *Division of work:* Specialization of labor is vital to attain organizational objectives.

2. *Authority:* The right to give orders must accompany responsibility.

3. *Discipline:* Obedience and respect ensure smooth running of an organization.

4. *Unity of command:* Ideally, each employee should report to only one superior.

5. *Unity of direction:* The efforts of everyone in the organization should be coordinated and focused in the same direction.

6. *Subordination of individual interests to the general interest:* Resolving the tug of war between personal and organizational interests in favor of the organization is one of management's greatest difficulties.

7. *Remuneration:* Employees should be paid fairly in accordance with their contribution

8. *Centralization:* The relationship between centralization and decentralization is a matter of proportion; the optimum balance must be found for each organization.

9. *Scalar chain:* Subordinates should observe the formal chain of command unless expressly authorized by their respective superiors to communicate with each other.

10. *Order:* Both material things and people should be in their proper places.

11. *Equity:* Fairness that results from a combination of kindliness and justice will lead to devoted and loyal service.

12. *Stability and tenure of personnel:* People need time to learn their jobs.

13. *Initiative:* One of the greatest satisfactions in formulating and carrying out a plan.

14. *Esprit de corps:* Harmonious effort among individuals is the key to organizational success.

Source: Ivancevich et al. *Management: Quality and Competitiveness, 2ⁿᵈ ed., Irwin, (Chicago and Boston), 1997.*

B.   *The Behavioral Approach*

The behavioral approach emphasizes individual needs (attitudes, behaviors, emotions, thoughts) within the organization. It shifts focus from the physical production-view of classical management to the social people-view of the work environment. In summary, this approach synthesizes both the human relations view and the organizational/behavioral science view. The human relations view argues that managers need to possess good Inter-personal skills since workers tend to respond more to the social context of their work environment. This in turn affects workers' productivity relative to their perception of the superior-subordinate relationship.

Two noted human relations theorists were Douglas McGregor and Abraham Maslow. McGregor developed theory X (a negative view of workers which underscored the classical approach) and theory Y (a positive view of workers which favored the human relations approach). Theory X assumes that people have an inherent dislike for work, disdain responsibility, and are afraid of entrepreneurial risk, but they prefer security and direction. Managerial control is, therefore, necessary to threaten, coerce, and direct employees to perform their functions. Theory Y assumes that people seek work as a natural part of their existence, are internally motivated and committed to seeking out and accepting responsibility, want to participate in organizational problem-solving, and often are under-utilized while getting less credit than they merit.

Another insight into motivation was developed by Abraham Maslow who identified the five need categories usually referred to as the "hierarchy of needs:"

Physiological – food, air, and water; guaranteed by adequate salary.

Safety – freedom from fear or harm, stability, Security; guaranteed by employment, health benefits, pension plan, etc.

Social – friendship, belongingness, camaraderie, teamwork; guaranteed by group membership and inclusion.

Esteem – status, sense of self-worth, job title; guaranteed by promotion or recognition.

Self-actualization – challenging job, personal growth and achievement of potential; guaranteed by participation in work decisions.

C.   *Organizational Behavior Approach*

Organizational behavior (OB) deals with the complex nature of human behavior in organizations more so than the human relations view. OB approaches human behavior in organizations from a multi-disciplinary and holistic perspective addressing not just the individual, but the group and the organization at large. It looks at issues such as leadership, group dynamics, power and politics, interpersonal conflict, motivation, organization structure, process and design. These affect an individual's psychological state and impact on one's job enrichment, sense of autonomy, and performance outcomes.

D. *Decision and Information Sciences Approach*

The decision and information sciences approach (also called the quantitative and/or management science approach) applies mathematics, statistics, operations management, information systems, computers and model building techniques in seeking precise solutions to business problems. Applicable areas are scheduling and selecting locations in addition to determining optimal economic quantities of supplies, inventory, storage, break-even analysis, etc.

E. *The Systems Approach*

The systems approach emphasizes the inter-relatedness or inter-dependence between the various parts of an organization. It looks at how events in one unit affect clinical outcomes in other units, and vice-versa. A typical example would be the extent to which delayed return of lab results could impact diagnosis, treatment plan, and patient outcome. Under this approach, organizations are viewed as systems. It enables managers to better understand their respective units or departments in relation to their level of inter-dependence with other units, departments, or even subsystems within their organization.

In the systems approach, decisions made by one manager may have far-reaching impacts on one or more departments of the organization.

An organization may also be viewed as an **Open System** or a **Closed System.** An open system interacts with, is sensitive to, and is linked with, its environment. One significant characteristic of the open system is that it is dynamic and progressive, so it easily adapts to market and other environmental forces. The open system lends itself to the traditional *Input, Process/ Transformation, Output model,* with continuous environmental feedback as shown below:

Figure 1: Input, Process, Output model

Unlike the closed system, the open system thrives in a less bureaucratic environment, and much more easily survives sudden organizational and environmental changes. The closed system by its nature is less adaptive, and thus not easily influenced by events in the external environment.

As a manager, therefore, you will need to see your unit as part of the total organization where every component of the system works in unison. Remember the common expression that the whole is greater than the sum of its parts.

F.   The Contingency Approach

The contingency approach, also called the situationalist

view, takes a multi-variate view to problem-solving, centering on the uniqueness of each situation, and not adopting the universalist view of the "one best way." Under the contingency view, a specific managerial behavior is contingent on a number of factors, some of which are: (1) the situation, (2) organizational structure, (3) resource availability—or lack thereof, (4) timing, (5) group or individual decision, (6) probable outcome and its impact, etc. Some other emerging contemporary issues that will continue to affect managerial behavior are the changing nature of work (telecommuting, computers and telecommunications technology), workforce diversity, employee participation, consumerism (discerning and highly informed consumers), regulatory/legal issues (e.g. tobacco, employee health and safety), ethics and social responsibility (environmental sensitivity), globalization and international security.

Tom Peters' nine principles of the best run companies, to some extent are reflective of the contingency approach. These principles will remain contemporary and applicable for a long time to come. They include:

- managing ambiguity and paradox;
- a bias for action;
- staying close to the customer;
- autonomy and entrepreneurship;
- productivity through people;
- being hands-on and value-driven;
- stick to the knitting by doing better that which you do best;
- simple form, lean staff by emphasizing few management layers;
- loose-tight properties by maintaining control while allowing staff relative flexibility

Source: Thomas J. Peters & Robert H. Waterman, Jr. (1982). *In Search of Excellence: Lessons from America's Best Run Companies, Warner Books, pp. 13 –14.*

The Functions of Management

A. *Planning*

Traditionally, the management process entails four basic activities—planning, organizing, leading, and controlling. Planning (which includes decision-making), is a primary and critical managerial function, hence it precedes the other three functions. Like other managers in different environments, the nurse-manager must understand the vision of his/her organization in order to more ably set goals and determine how best to attain them. Planning encompasses environmental scanning, identifying the organization's mission and goals as well as the rationale for those goals, resource acquisition and allocation, understanding constraints, and setting time-lines and courses of action for accomplishment.

The nurse-manager's ability to plan or make decisions will certainly be affected by time constraints, available information, limited resources, organizational culture and complexity, collateral impact, personal needs, and many other unforeseen factors. This is commonly referred to as *bounded rationality.*

Essentials of a good Plan

A good plan begins with the end in mind. It must be specific with clearly defined objectives, and should fit into the overall mission of the organization. Without sacrificing stability, it should anticipate possible future conditions and provide for environmental flexibility. Good plans are also realistic, attainable, time-specific, cost effective and result in measurable outcomes based on clear pre-set standards.

Within the patient care environment it is important that the nurse-manager be aware of hospital-wide plans, is empowered to offer inputs, and is willing to implement such plans within the context of unit goals which are in consonance with institutional goals. It is, therefore, desirable for nurse-managers to understand and be sensitive to the factors that affect planning, such as funds, personnel, competitors, government legislation and the regulatory environment, economic and social conditions, technology, and industry/professional standards. The illustration below identifies the internal and external constituents that affect the nurse-manager's functions, and impact upon patient care delivery:

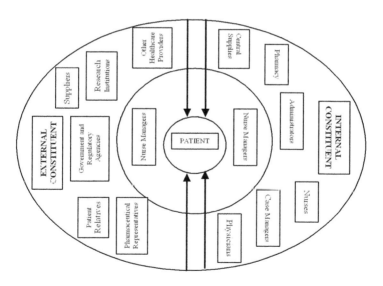

Figure 2: Constituents Affecting the Nurse-Manager's Functions

Steps In the Planning Process

Steps in the planning process are indeed synonymous with the decision-making process. Traditional management literature outlines this process as:

- Recognizing or identifying problems—or opportunities—and setting measuring parameters or standards. This will enable you to set organizational goals: for example, capturing a specific percentage of the health care market within a given geographical area, improving or attaining an identified patient satisfaction level, decreasing medication error rate, or becoming a regional leader in a particular healthcare specialty, etc.

- Determining priorities relative to the problems or opportunities. This will be affected by present and future conditions impacting on the problems or opportunities. For example, what critical variables come into play, especially following analysis of strengths, weaknesses, opportunities and threats? Critical variables may be heightened patient awareness regarding their health, new health insurance guidelines or regulations, competition, biomedical and technological advancements requiring employee retraining, limited capital resources, and dwindling patient census.

- Developing alternative means or courses of action. This will involve a systematic approach to problem solving. Questions such as who does what, when, how, and why, will need to be answered for each course of action.

- Evaluating the alternative means or courses of action using identifiable cost/benefit benchmarks.

- Selecting and implementing the least cost/optimum value alternative or set of alternatives.

- Evaluating outcomes and taking remedial actions, if and when necessary.

Plan Range

Planning may be for short-range, intermediate-range, or long-range. Short-range plans usually cover 0-1 year (dealing more with day-to-day operational issues such as scheduling, care-plans, and orientation). Intermediate-range plans cover a period of 1-3 years (dealing with things such as moving to a new clinic within the same location or some type of employee on-the-job-training). Long-range plans cover a period of 3-5 years or even longer (e.g. equipment needs, facilities expansion, and strategic positioning). While nurse-managers should be knowledgeable about all three types of plan range, they will spend more time dealing with problems arising out of events in the short-range.

B.   Organizing

Organizing involves a systematic *grouping* of tasks and resources in addition to *identifying* of authority relationships within a formal structure or framework. This ensures that a manager would have specific authority to supervise a group of employees, their jobs, and their tasks. In organizations, some functions are primary and directly tied to the basic mission, while others are secondary or support functions. In a hospital or medical institution, functions may be broadly divided into **clinical** services (medical—all branches—and nursing), **allied health services** (medical records or patient information system, pharmacy, physical, occupational and speech therapy); **diagnostic services** (laboratory, x-ray); **administrative** (top management, human resources, business services); **auxiliary services** (food services, housekeeping, security, plant maintenance/grounds-keeping, counseling and pastoral services). It is important to ensure an optimal mix and utilization of these resources (inputs) for the best outcomes, recognizing that in a medical institution, a satisfied patient should be the ultimate outcome. The patient care model below illustrates the expected outcomes.

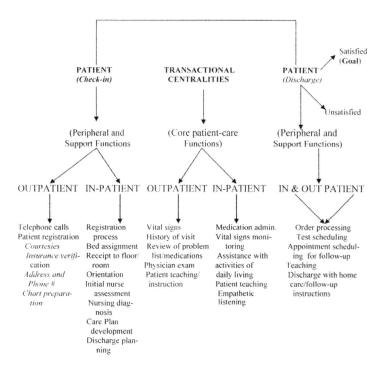

Figure 3:   *Patient-centered Care Model*

The above model summarizes some activities that take place in a typical patient encounter—whether "In" or "Out." Patient care delivery must be organized in such a way as to ensure patient satisfaction. Thus, the manner in which every activity within this model is carried out is critical. A satisfied patient is more likely to return, and also to spread the good word about the clinic's services. In like manner, an unsatisfied patient will not only seek another provider, but will spread negative information to prospective patients, thereby further reducing the clinic's competitiveness and market share.

To ensure an optimal mix of resources for the best outcomes means having the appropriate doctor-patient and nurse-patient ratios, having the right quantity and quality of medical supplies and equipment for a projected patient volume and patient acuity and having an efficient patient data-base and appropriate levels of administrative/clerical support. The nurse-manager who desires to organize efficiently and effectively must, therefore, be sensitive to organizational events and their impact on his/her operating environment. For example, a sudden rise in patient census and patient acuity will put pressure on clinical resources which challenges the nurse-manager's management skills.

C.   Leading

Leading is the management function by which managers influence subordinates by instilling in them the vision, values, and expectations of their organization. Leaders create and provide a nurturing environment that enables others to excel. Those who aspire to positions of leadership must embrace the spirit of servanthood. No one has put the concept of servanthood in better perspective than Rick Warren in his book "The Purpose Driven Life". He states that:

"Thousands of books have been written on leadership, but few on servanthood. Everyone wants to lead; no one wants to be a servant. We would rather be generals than privates. Jesus specialized in menial tasks that everyone else tried to avoid: washing feet, helping children, fixing breakfast, and serving lepers... (1) Real servants make themselves available to serve (2) Real servants pay attention to needs (3)

Real servants are faithful to their ministry (4) Real servants maintain a low profile. "

Source: *Rick Warren, "The Purpose Driven Life", Zondervan , (2002) p.257-258, p.260*

In the words of John Wesley, "Do all the good you can, by all the means you can, in all the ways you can, in all the places you can, at all the times you can, to all the people you can, as long as you ever can." Through vicarious leadership, a manager can expect subordinate commitment to organizational goals.

An effective leader:
- makes job expectations clear
- leads by example
- supports his/her subordinates in their observance of work rules
- cautiously and gently criticizes the job not the person
- is understanding and considerate, yet firm
- provides prompt feedback to employees on their performance
- knows when, how, and what level of reward or punishment to give
- seeks the personal and professional growth of subordinates.
- is a good listener
- is fair, just, and impartial in the application of rules and regulations

Differentiating management from leadership:

- People don't want to be managed
- They want to be led
- Whoever heard of a world manager?
- World leader, yes
- Educational leader
- Political leader
- Religious leader
- Community leader
- Labor leader
- Business leader – they all lead, they don't manage
- The carrot always wins over the stick
- Ask your horse; you can lead your horse to water, but you can't manage him to drink!
- If you want to manage somebody, manage yourself
- Do that well and you'll be ready to stop managing— and start leading.

Source: Warren Bennis and Burt Nannus, *Leaders: The Strategies for Taking Charge* (New York: Harper & Row, 1985), p.22.

John Gardner, former secretary of the US Department of Health, Education and Welfare, and a frontline writer on leadership, states that leaders/managers:

1. Think longer-term, beyond the daily crises

2. Grasp their unit's relationship to the bigger organizational picture—their overall organization industry trends, and so forth.

3. Reach constituents beyond their own department's boundaries, such as suppliers and customers.

4. Emphasize intangibles of vision, values, and motivation to work with, and understand, people.
5. Have political skill in coping with conflicting requirements of multiple stake-holders, such as other departments, customers, suppliers, unions, and top management.

6. Think in terms of renewal

Source: John W. Gardner, *On Leadership* (New York: Free Press, 1990), p.4

In summary, genuine leadership entails being a visionary and an innovator. It is an accepted axiom that the only thing constant about change is change itself. An effective leader must therefore anticipate, plan for, be ready to accept, and implement change. Only those who can truly inspire and direct others in the relentless pursuit of excellence will ultimately be great leaders.

D. *Controlling/Evaluating*

Controlling/evaluating is the management function of monitoring and assessing planned activities to ascertain whether or not set objectives have been attained. For example, a hospital may establish that 98% of the patients coming through its emergency room must be attended to within ten minutes of their arrival. If only 85% of such patients are attended to within ten minutes in a given period, then the objective is not met. Reasons—e.g. patient acuity, personnel shortage—must be stated for such failure, and remedial measures put in place. Ideally, control involves identifying and setting performance standards, defining measurement methods, measuring actual performance, comparing performance against standards, identifying alternative corrective steps, selecting and implementing the best corrective step, and continuous monitoring. Like other managers, the nurse-manager in his/her management of resources must strive to be both effective and efficient. Effectiveness simply is the attainment of set objectives, while efficiency is attaining objectives in a cost-effective way. Mosley, Pietri and Megginson (1996) aptly illustrate this in their effectiveness-efficiency matrix:

HIGH **EFFECTIVENESS**	Objective(s) met or exceeded; wasted resources	Objective(s) met or exceeded; resources well used
LOW	Objective(s) not reached; wasted resources	Objective(s) not reached; resources well used
	LOW　　　　**EFFICIENCY**　　　　HIGH	

Figure 4: Effectiveness-Efficiency Matrix

Source: Mosley et al., Management: Leadership In Action; 5th edition, New York: HarperCollins College Publishers, 1996, p.584

To ensure effective evaluation, goals must be specific, measurable, attainable, realistic and time-sensitive.

Kinds of Managers

Traditionally, there are three levels of management: the executive (top) level, the middle level, and the first-line. Top level management includes the chief executive officer (usually the president, chairman/CEO), vice-presidents, and division heads. While this group is few in number, they provide strategic direction, determine organizational expansion and contraction, set the tone for others to follow, and are responsible to the Board of Directors.

Middle level managers are department heads, who are responsible for carrying out the plans of top management. They supervise and coordinate the functions of first-line managers. First-line managers are supervisors such as foremen, office managers, head nurses, unit leaders, etc. These people coordinate the activities of operating employees.

Managerial Roles

Management theorists have identified three major managerial roles: interpersonal, informational, and decisional. **Interpersonal** roles involve working and interacting with, and understanding people within and without the organization. In an interpersonal role, a manager may function as a:

- *figurehead* (ceremonial representative of his/her organization at public or social functions);

- *leader* (motivator, visionary, encourager); and

- *liaison* (linkage between the organization and its employees or between the organization and external constituents).

Informational roles deal with receipt, storage, retrieval and movement of information. In this role, a manager may function as a

- *monitor* (scanning the environment for information)

- *disseminator* (communicates or circulates information among subordinates or fellow managers)

- *spokesperson* (moving information from the organization to outsiders).

Decisional roles involve making a choice among different courses of action. In this role the manager acts as

- *entrepreneur* (innovator of new products, ideas or processes);

- *disturbance handler/Negotiator* (mediator, arbitrator of conflicts among employees or units, negotiates contracts);

- *resource allocator* (distributes resources among units in accordance with organizational plans).

Managerial Skills

Skill is activated or applied knowledge. Traditionally, managerial skills are categorized into **conceptual** (cognitive ability, reasoning at a high level); **technical** (practical, skill-based, necessary to understand tasks); and **human/ interpersonal** (also called people- skills: ability to work with and motivate people in order to influence their behavior). Other important managerial skills are **analytical** (identifying how pieces of the organizational puzzle fit together); **diagnostic** (ability to predict causes by analyzing symptoms); **decision-making** (ability to recognize or define problems or opportunities, and to choose the best option); **communication**

skills (ability to convey and receive verbal and nonverbal ideas and information); **computer skills** (ability to use the computer in formulating, accessing or circulating information) and **time-management skills** (ability to prioritize activities and to assign or delegate functions). While each skill is important at all levels of management, the relative importance of any skill may be a function of the level of administrative or operational responsibility. For example, the higher the level, the more conceptual, analytical, diagnostic and time-management skills are required.

Dealing With Employees

At whatever level of management, employee issues rank among one of the most sensitive in organizations, especially when they involve privacy. Do not pry into employees' private lives, unless they **first** seek your input.

If you are concerned that an employee's off-work behavior will adversely affect their work performance, make sure that there are written guidelines that address that issue. Be certain that all employees are given copies, informed about it, and required to sign off as evidence of their knowledge of the guidelines. It is also important to always consult the department of human resources when you have questions or are in doubt.

Many employees are commonly concerned about their perception of their supervisor's fairness. As a manager, strive to be even-handed in granting rewards or enforcing punishment. For performance appraisals, make sure that employees are aware of established written and measurable standards of performance. Avoid emotional *"feel good"* recommendations; for instance, do not recommend any unmerited raises or praise poor performance for fear the employee may feel bad. You cannot document enough on the profile of employee performance, including antecedent actions or behavior such as lateness to work, abuse of sick days, substandard work, patient complaints, fellow employee complaints, long coffee breaks, etc.

Other guidelines for performance appraisal objectivity include the following:

- do not be biased (one way or the other) toward an employee;

- evaluate the employee's performance skills against measurable job requirements;

- employees with similar job titles and performing same jobs should be evaluated on the same criteria;

- each evaluation criterion should be analyzed independently and not *"piggy-backed;"*

- apply the "golden rule"—given the same set of conditions, would you be willing to be evaluated similarly?

- promptly provide the employee with performance feedback;

- the overall evaluation should take into account the interests of the employee, the appraiser, and the organization in a fair, just and impartial manner. It is improper for a manager not to be open to an employee in matters involving the employee's performance as a first step in helping that employee to improve or overcome their deficiencies.

CHAPTER 3
TIME MANAGEMENT

One of the topics that gets frequent attention in organizations is time management—and rightly so, as the manager's role is loaded with numerous functions. For example, as a nurse manager you play the role of teacher, counselor, patient advocate and, sometimes, family intermediary. Your stakeholder base includes not only the patient, but his/her family, subordinates, superiors, fellow employees, and customers outside your organization. It is important that your repertoire of skills include time management to enable you attend to the needs of this diverse populace.

Time management involves prioritizing your activities in such a way as to maximize the work time at your disposal in order to accomplish organizational and personal objectives. Prioritizing enables you to sort your tasks/duties. Some people categorize or rank such tasks/duties according to their level of relative importance - the *most important, more important, and important,* the *most urgent, more urgent, and urgent.* In some cases, a combination of these elements may also be applied, i.e. *most important and most urgent* (critical); *important and urgent* (moderate attention); *important but not urgent* (not time sensitive). These elements are explicitly outlined by Dr. Stephen R. Covey in his Time Management Matrix.

	Urgent	Not Urgent

Important	**I**
	Crises
	Pressing problems
	Deadline-driven
	  projects, meetings
	  preparations
		II
		Preparation
		Prevention
		Values clarification
		Planning
		Relationship building
		Needed relaxation
		Empowerment

Not Important	Needless interruptions
	Unnecessary reports
	Unimportant meetings,
	  phone calls, mail
	Other people's minor
	  issues
	
	III
		Trivia, busywork
		Some phone calls
		Time wasters
		"Escape" activities
		Irrelevant mail
		Excessive TV
		Excessive relaxation
		IV

Figure 5:   Time Management Matrix

Source: Steven Covey: "The 7 Habits of Highly Effective People: Powerful Lessons in Personal Change, p. 151, published by Simon & Schuster. (Fireside Books), New York, 1990.

According to Covey, Quadrant II elements are often neglected because their importance is minimized by their non-urgency (not time sensitive). However, understanding and applying these elements are essential to the development of effective time management.

Categorizing or classifying your tasks will enable you to identify those primary functions that you will accord immediate attention or perform by yourself, and those secondary functions you may want to delegate to subordinates. Effective delegation will save you from early burnout and frustration due to task overload, and also afford your subordinates the opportunity to be trained, groomed, and developed.

One of the keys to effective time management is maintaining a *"daily planner"*—simply a regular calendar to enable you track your appointments and/or things to do. Some *planners* are simple, while others are more complex. Regardless of your preference, the typical planner contains the month and days of the week, arranged hourly or half-hourly. Some have spaces or additional pages for addresses and telephone numbers.

It is important that you stick to the entries in your *planner* as much as possible. Having a good *planner* that you may never use is as good as having none. To ensure that they stick to their *planners,* some people maintain two *planners*—one at the office and one at home. A standard calendar at home will suffice to complement your office *planner.*

One of the elements that impacts time management is procrastination—the tendency to keep putting things off. Some managers, consciously or unconsciously, let things pile up in their "In" tray or on their table, and all over the floor. The effect is that they remain overwhelmed with a sense of overload so they look constantly frazzled and disorganized. They are always trying to "catch up" but they never do, and are left feeling like they are in a gun battle while armed with a knife! This leads to inefficiency and ineffectiveness. They soon begin to lose the respect of subordinates, peers and superiors, especially if their employees' work flow depends upon the completion of the manager's tasks. Such managers miss deadlines, are always forgetful, and can neither inspire nor motivate others. As a result, they drum up excuse after excuse in their attempt to justify their lapses.

Procrastination is overcome by being perceptive, proactive, and performance-oriented. Being able to prioritize, delegate, follow-up, and treat issues as they arise will go a long way to ensure effective time management. Be adept also at using modern communication technology facilities. Wireless access has become commonplace. Good time managers take personal responsibility and are accountable; they continually seek better and more efficient ways of doing things. They are also self-driven with zeal to accomplish goals and meet deadlines. They readily admit and correct their errors. They embark on periodic self-evaluations, focusing on their core functions or position while streamlining emerging functions.

A final note – be your own time manager. Don't let tasks and time manage you. Energy spent on good planning is not a waste. Lack of planning gives birth to disorderliness, and disorderliness to inertia, ultimately leading to a dead organization. Remember, time as an organizational resource is both finite and elusive. You must be creative in maximizing it for personal and organizational benefits.

CHAPTER 4
LEADERSHIP TRAITS AND STYLE

The Challenge

A s healthcare organizations face competition, regulatory changes, and revolution in bio-medical technology, healthcare leaders must embark on strategies to ensure long-term organizational survival and sustainability. The challenge is also compounded by an increasingly diverse, more educated and technically competent workforce along with the tendency toward leaner organizations.

As we move from the era of job security to financial security, from a production to a service orientation, and from structured knowledge to dynamic learning, employees are going to demand a more flexible, participative and outcome-oriented leadership. According to Mosley, Pietri and Megginson (1996), *"Leading* will require greater use of motivational tactics designed for creativity, achievement, prestige, and self-expression; more emphasis on personal dignity and worth, security, recognition; and participation; and improved communication, especially upwards."[2] This tendency toward *organizational liberalism* (or *managed structure*) however, would not mean an end to, or absence of, the traditional structure. Hopefully, leaders will continue to provide vision that will define and shape an organization's goals as well as create a nurturing and motivating environment for the accomplishment of those goals.

Leadership Traits

Over the years, management theorists and psychologists have debated the nature-nurture question in terms of leadership traits as opposed to actual leadership behavior. While trait theories focus on a leader's personal drives and characteristics, behavioral theories focus on what a leader actually does. Ultimately, behavior is driven by motivation which in turn may be influenced by an individual's predisposition toward certain traits. Leaders should possess certain traits or characteristics such as:

- **Truthfulness:** The ability to be sincere to oneself and to others in an abiding faith in what is right, noble, honest and enduring. It involves being candid, principle-centered, and standing for what is incontrovertible, accurate, correct and verifiable. Truth spares you the unpleasant effects of fatal illusions. Nothing can be more demoralizing to your subordinates than perceiving you as untruthful, unreliable and dishonest. If you are a standard bearer of truth in your organization, even your detractors and stubborn subordinates will attest (albeit behind you!) that *"though he/she is firm, at least they are honest. They let you know where they stand."*

- **Fairness:** This is the ability to be just, impartial, rational and unprejudiced in decision-making. A good manager avoids making emotionally-based decisions.

- **Dependability:** In game five of the 1997 NBA

championship between the *Chicago Bulls* and *Utah Jazz,* Michael Jordan proved dependable in spite of his illness by leading his team to a win that virtually assured their likelihood of clinching the championship in game six. The true leader is like the captain who refuses to *abandon* ship until all

- the ship's passengers are safe ashore.

- **Professionalism:** This characteristic encompasses expertise, sense of duty, attention to detail, and respect for what is desirable, honorable and ethical. Professionalism would also require that you develop and share with your subordinates (and superiors) your personal mission statement. An ideal personal mission statement should seek to be congruent with unit and organizational mission and objectives, otherwise it may be time to part! One of the authors has the following personal and unit mission statements:

PERSONAL MISSION: *To model and foster principle-centered leadership that is based on truth and fairness and empowers people to grow and be productive.*

UNIT MISSION: *We are committed to creating and fostering a quality health care environment with a shared vision of superior service to our customers, organizational achievement, and personal growth. Our mission is comprised of the following interrelated parts:*

A. *The Patient: To deliver individualized quality primary health care to all our patients with a personal touch.*

B. *Organization: To contribute towards organizational effectiveness and efficiency through constructive resource allocation and utilization, and inter- and intra-departmental cooperation in support of the center's mission of patient care, education, and research.*

C. *Psychosocial:* *To instill in primary care employees a sense of shared values that will promote a healthy work environment and provide opportunities for personal, professional, and institutional growth.*

- **Versatility:** The ability to turn with ease from one thing to another. This trait enables a leader to respond quickly to change.

- **Sensitivity:** The ability to be aware of the needs and emotions of others. The need for this trait cannot be overemphasized. As a leader, you need to be seen as caring and empathetic. It is as important in dealing with staff as it is in dealing with patients and their significant others. An atmosphere of understanding and trust is very crucial to employee motivation and loyalty. This would enable you to steer them toward a course that would meet their professional and personal growth needs, your own needs, and the needs of the organization.

- **Commitment:** The state of being obligated or emotionally impelled. If the leader is committed to the cause of the organization/unit, the followers are more likely to do the same.

- **Integrity:** The state of being complete or undivided in one's adherence to a code of moral values. Integrity begets trust and respect in relation to superiors, peers, and subordinates. Character can also be a function of integrity.

- **Creativity/Initiative:** Ability to generate ideas and preempt solutions to actual and perceived problems. A creative leader is always innovative—constantly seeking ways to do things better.

- **Decisiveness:** The ability to proceed with an action (once decision is made) in a swift, prompt, certain, and competent manner—guided by integrity and thorough comprehension of all pieces of the *puzzle*

- **Patience/Stress Tolerance:** The ability and willingness to calmly endure hardship or trials. It can be deemed as maintaining internal peace and decorum under pressure or turbulence. Some theorists refer to this as having a sense of self-assurance, or self-confidence. Others may regard it as emotional intelligence. Remember, your subordinates are looking up to you, and their perception of how you handle stressful situations will affect their depth of reliance on you as a leader.

A good leader is one who is constantly searching for ways to optimize both productivity and stakeholder satisfaction. A leader who clarifies expected outcomes, simplifies tasks, provides support and a facilitating environment, and establishes a reward system that is uniformly applied, will go a long way in molding subordinate behavior toward accomplishment of organizational goals. Good leaders do not command or coerce obedience; they influence followership. Under a respected leader, followers or subordinates see duty as a joy not a burden.

Leadership Styles

The Path-Goal Theory of Leadership deals with "four leadership styles and several contingency factors leading to three indicators of leader effectiveness" (McShane and Von Glinow, 2005). The four leadership styles are *directive, supportive, participative* and *achievement-oriented. Directive leadership* is task-oriented, a feature of an authoritarian environment. *Supportive leadership* is more *coaching* oriented, providing subordinates opportunities to learn, while assuring leader support in the event of need. *Achievement-oriented leadership* encourages subordinates to attempt and excel at challenging tasks, and links subordinate rewards to levels of achievement. *Participative leadership* makes for *consultative democracy* in the work place and seeks worker input; but ultimate decision rests with the leader or manager. It is different from situations where decision is made either by consensus or by majority.

McShane and Von Glinow (2005) further state that leader effectiveness is influenced by (1) employee contingencies – skill levels and experience, and locus of control; (2) environmental contingencies – task structure and team dynamics; and (3) leader contingencies in terms of how the leader creates an environment that promotes employee motivation, employee satisfaction, and acceptance of the leader (hierarchy of authority/power).

For purposes of simplicity and the practical basis upon which this book is written, the above concepts are further analyzed in terms of autocratic or democratic leadership styles. Of course, there are elements between these extremes that make one more or less preferable. These patterns are commonly identified in Management literature as follows:

A. Autocratic

1. *Exploitative-Authoritative:* This is characterized by centralized decision-making, task orientation, and the use of coercion and threats of punishment to ensure subordinate compliance. While this method may have its place, it is not common in modern organizations, but rather a relic from classical management theory. It can be applied in cases where subordinate behavior is dependent, time is of the essence, and resource loss would be catastrophic in the event of a mishap. While it makes for faster decisions, implementation often gets stalled because subordinates see themselves only as "programmed robots" who lack intellectual skill, and who can only accomplish functions by being externally manipulated or controlled.

2. *Benevolent-Authoritative:* This is characterized by pervasive *management by exception* whereby major policy decisions are made by top-level management, and operational-type decisions are left to lower-level management. It has a thinly veiled trace of *delegated* paternalism (embellished *"empowerment"*), which leaves subordinates feeling like "overgrown kindergarteners." Subordinates are compelled to implement decisions essentially on a selfish motive, because of the perceived (extrinsic-induced) benefits that may trickle down from top management.

B.   Democratic:

1.   *Consultative:* This is characterized by bottom-up decision-making, whereby top management makes a conscious effort to solicit input from lower level management. Usually, the manager makes a decision with the option to use or not use the input from subordinates. This gives subordinates a sense of inclusion, even though their inputs may not be used.

2.   *Participative:* This allows for inputs from organizational members, though ultimate decision rests with management. This style offers employees a sense of empowerment, and is often a training ground for future managers. While the manager remains accountable, subordinates support decision implementation usually as a result of some feeling of intrinsic motivation.

3.   *Consensus:* This goes beyond consultation and participation; the goal is unanimity or majority of opinion in decision making. It lends itself to a sense of collective responsibility and group- think.

C.   Laisse-faire Leadership

This can be characterized as a liberal leadership style, whereby a leader or manager somewhat applies a *"hands-off"* approach in dealing with subordinates. This approach may be appropriate in situations where subordinates are seasoned, mature, self-directed individuals who need less directive leadership. It may also be suitable in very stable environments where decisions are programmed.

D. *Situational Leadership*

There is another type of leader often referred to in management literature—the situational leader. The concept of the situational leader is based on the assumption that irrespective of the individual leader's personality, leader response is contingent on the situation or context. Specific leader response or behavior may be influenced by situational urgency, decision significance, leader propensity toward risk/ risk aversion, and logistical resources.

In conclusion, effective leadership calls for:

- continuous and objective self-assessment

- ability to recruit and develop competent subordinates (literally *cloning* oneself),

- empathetic listening and being available to your team

- standing for the truth

- willingness to accept and remedy the leader's own deficiencies

- being optimistic

- ability to preempt and plan for the future

- willingness to take constructive risks.

CHAPTER 5
POLITICS AND ORGANIZATIONAL
CULTURE

The truth about organizational behavior is that employees, regardless of level, are inescapably interdependent in their functional and psycho-social relationships in the work place. Some work situations may give rise to conflicts and cliques ("us versus them"), while others may engender concourse and compromise.

Generally speaking, the word *"politics"* scares many people because it is often synonymous with being *"dirty"*, sneaky, cunning, crafty, and contriving. Politics, whether in the traditional sense of national governance or in the parochial sense of organizations, is a fact of life. There are those who govern and those who are governed, in addition to the powerful and the not so powerful—or even the powerless. We live in a world in which those who have power or are in control do not voluntarily give it up. Consequently, government, business, and social institutions have laws and regulations to check the human propensity toward the excessive use and abuse of power. Even then, individuals and groups must contend with those in power on a daily basis. Sometimes the *right* people are in power; at other times there are *low* people in *high* places!

Inasmuch as the *political game* is played at all levels, your formal position in an organization determines the nature of your political fights. Senior or top level management direct the strategic vision of the organization and have *global* decision making powers. They also influence resource acquisition, control, and allocation (including coercive and reward powers) in addition to acting as organizational spokespersons. Intermediate level managers exercise power over resource use, manage immediate subordinate (line) personnel, assert technical expertise, propagate the centrality of their departments, and seek powerful access through productivity and reward manipulation. Lower level managers (supervisors or forepersons) acquire political influence through technical expertise, effective mentoring of operatives, and access to primary information (especially if such information is central to the organization's survival such as marketing demographics and sources of raw materials). Let us now discuss some of the factors that may form the basis for a manager's power in an organization.

A manager's *position* in the organization's formal hierarchy: different positions attract different levels of respect, recognition or power, even when the individuals in those positions are unaware of the "power that goes with the territory."

Information power: This results from one's access to very important or sensitive information, the divulging of which could alter the course of events in an organization. Healthcare employees deal with information affecting patient and employee confidentiality on a daily basis. Flippant comments that lead to conscious or unconscious divulging of confidential information must be avoided.

Expertise: This comes from one's professional competence/ technical skills, specialized knowledge in a field or discipline, e.g. physician, lawyer, or engineer. As a Nurse-Manager, it may be your IV (intra-venous) skills, ability to triage, or interpersonal communication skills with patients as well as employees. Being an expert at something does not necessarily mean that you are perfect at it. It means that you possess a thorough or higher level of mastery, with slim or unlikely chances of making mistakes usually common among average performers in that field. As a manager, your expertise may also come from your ability to resource the right answers outside the immediate spheres of your own competence. This is very important, because subordinates and superiors alike depend on you to have the *right* answers – or know where to get them!

Charisma: This is often called referent power, and is based on a manager's individual traits and/or characteristics that people find appealing, noteworthy, or desirable. Sometimes, charisma may be inexplicable; hence you may hear an employee say, "I just like manager X, but I cannot explain why." While a manager's charisma may be endearing, it may not equally appeal to all employees across the board. A charismatic manager may also be *affective.* This characteristic results from a manager's ability to:

- empathize with, and motivate employees,
- be sensitive to the feelings of his/her stakeholders,
- meaningfully *reach out* from the *managerial ivory tower* to attend to the common concerns of others; the non-isolationist manager can be seen readily *hand-shaking, flesh pressing,* and interacting freely with employees and customers. Bob Tillman, president and CEO of Lowe's states that "we make people from headquarters wear aprons when they visit" Lowe's stores, because "there's only one reason to be in a store, and that's to help the customers."

Source: (The Dallas Morning News, November 2, 1997, Homing in on customers: article by Cheryl Hall*).*

Centrality: This refers to how close one is to a power base. For instance, the secretary or administrative assistant to the Chief Executive Officer (CEO) of a major organization may have, or is perceived to have, more (associative) power or "gate-keeper" influence than a typical middle level manager simply due to access to the CEO. While you may not have power, your access to the power source or to the corridor of power can make you a *power player or broker.*

Whatever the type of power one may possess, it should be remembered that the primary purpose of such power is to accomplish a task, and to apply this power for the ultimate and utmost good of those served—whether an organization or individuals.

Nurses and Power-play

By their very nature—perhaps due to their training—nurses are less prone to playing the "power" game in the work place. As a manager, you must strive to survive in a work environment where there is competition for resources. You also need to appropriately align yourself, and develop a network for survival. One mistake often made by new managers is the sense that they will be readily accepted in their new environment. While position power results from structural relationships in organizations, political power may often result from one's strategic posture within the intricate network or web of those who wield decision-making influence. However, there is a caveat—misuse and unconscionable manipulation of political power may come back to haunt their perpetrators some day.

First Things First

Some tips are important. First, you must understand and identify with the mission and vision of your organization. Second, understand how your department fits into that mission and vision. Third, observe the social network in both your immediate unit and other units—know the individuals and the specific roles they play, and know which roles are primary or central to the organization's survival. Fourth, identify an interdisciplinary social group that you feel will meet your social, professional and personal growth needs. This is critical because it may determine your support system and your preferred mentor. Remember, you are in your job primarily for economic well-being, contribution to your organization, and personal psycho-social enrichment.

Power Sharing

No one person has all the answers to workplace problems—or any problem for that matter. An effective manager knows that he/she has to share some aspects of their power in order to ensure organizational survival. Power sharing through delegation, decentralization, consultation and group participation makes employees feel like an integral part of the system. It also increases employee morale, loyalty and commitment. Two major aspects of power sharing deserve mention: empowerment and liberation.

Empowerment involves delegating power or authority to your subordinates. It can increase employee motivation and the total amount of power in the organization. Elements of empowerment include information sharing, enlisting employee knowledge and skills in problem solving, and establishing a reinforcement and reward program based on performance.

Liberation goes a little further than empowerment. While empowerment may be somewhat limited in scope, it denotes *king/subject*, *boss/subordinate*, *powerful/powerless* relationships. Liberation allows employees more *elbow room* to make some substantive or autonomous decisions related to their functional areas. Liberation entails organizational freedom, accountability, and responsibility. It unleashes an employee's entrepreneurial and creative/innovative energy. It fosters a state of mind whereby the employee feels their future prosperity is a function of the organization's growth and survival. Liberation management enables employees to:

- identify with the organization's goals and objectives
- cultivate initiative
- see themselves as "organizational ambassadors"
- seek avenues for expanding their professional knowledge in order to better serve their organization and clientele

- be driven by excellence and quality in their daily tasks

- feel happy going to work.

Enriched by a high level of employee maturity, experience and expertise, and accompanied by top management's vision, commitment and openness to *evolutionary* and *progressive* ideas, liberation management can flourish in an atmosphere of complete trust.

Regardless of the approach used for power sharing, caution should be exercised to ensure that both the employees and the organization benefit by way of increased morale and increased productivity. In the healthcare environment, the nurse-manager must remember that the patient is the focus.

Plans for employee *empowerment* must thus be balanced with an employee's level of clinical competence and commitment to organizational mission. Healthcare decisions in the hands of an amateur can have far-reaching consequences.

We have some more notes regarding empowerment. Organizations must avoid *passive patronage* or what is often referred to as *paternalism*. This involves outward pretence of empowerment that does not exist in practice. In other words, the organization pays lip-service to empowerment. It does not reflect well on an organization's leadership if employees perceive empowerment as a joke or mere gimmick. According to Thomas Petzinger, "empowering workers only patronizes them; brain work should be a duty, not an indulgence. In addition, brain work requires rules—the fewer the better, but enough to assure that ideas turn into action."

Source: *(Wall Street Journal, "Forget Empowerment, This Job Requires Constant Brainpower", October 17, 1997)*

As you assume managerial or supervisory responsibilities, study your new environment very carefully and be cautious in introducing changes. Remember, just like a new born baby, you have to be fed with liquid food before solid food. You will learn to sit, crawl, stand, walk, and then run. You risk failure if you attempt to do all at the same time. It is very critical that you lay a sound and solid foundation upon which to *build* later. This period of adjustment essentially introduces you to the *politics* of your new environment. It is, therefore, important that you begin to build your credibility from day one by the way you compose yourself, by your knowledge or expertise of your job, by your interpersonal skills, and by your willingness to learn. It is important that you attract the respect of your peers, the allegiance of your subordinates and trust of your superiors. Associate with those who have creative energy and ideas that can be _realistically_ harnessed. It is not unusual to have fellow employees who have a lot of _good and grandiose,_ but _impractical_ ideas.

Remember, politics is not only the art and science of government; it is also the art and know-how of survival in an ever competitive and, sometimes, hostile organizational environment. A few tips may be helpful:

- _Do some social "mapping":_ Social mapping is used here to denote efforts at identifying key and influential people in your organization, and particularly in your department. Such people usually have a certain level of access not otherwise available to the average person or employee in the organization. They can become handy or useful in the future, especially as you seek other opportunities. A point of caution, however, is necessary. Strive to maintain a cautious distance and establish your own identity through a track record of performance and personal accomplishments. Remember, power does change hands, and so do the players. If you are tied inextricably to the apron strings of current power brokers, when the tide changes, you may be swept aside. In the final analysis, while _power association_ is desirable, your excellent performance may become your anchor after the change of the _guards._ To some extent, social mapping will enable you to understand your organization's culture.

- _Be an Optimist:_ Nobody likes a pessimist, a complainer or worrier. Visionary management always looks for those who possess a positive attitude.

- *Do Strategic Positioning:* Networking begins at your work environment. Be active in organization-wide activities, even on a voluntary basis such as participating in problem-solving task forces or committees. It is also crucial that you get to know your co-workers as they are often your single most important source of job-related information. In establishing your peer network, consider widening your horizon, as you seek to know people on similar levels from other departments and from outside organizations. Strategic positioning may involve preemptive solution to potential problems in and outside your functional area. Your solutions may lower costs, increase productivity, improve process, and thus enhance your unit's importance and your organization's bottom line. It may also increase your centrality, and somewhat render you almost indispensable to your organization.

- *Be professionally active:* Join professional associations, nationwide and locally. Attend seminars/workshops regularly, and consider writing articles in professional journals. In other words, stay abreast of the trends in your profession.

- *Act as a Professional:* Model excellence, self-respect, and professional integrity. In your dealings, especially with your subordinates, treat people with courtesy. To truly enjoy a happy work environment, you need to have a cordial work and personal relationship with your crew.

- *Offer Realistic Reinforcement:* Acknowledge your subordinates, and promptly praise them for good performance. Do not, however, give blind or undue praise; otherwise you may be unintentionally reinforcing mediocrity. One other disadvantage of such meaningless praise is that it makes realistic evaluation difficult during actual performance appraisal of your subordinate(s). But deserved praise is certainly like a *breath of fresh air,* and is to be encouraged. For poor performance, attempt to identify and harness the potential in the person while offering remedial guidance.

- *Use the "Grapevine":* From time to time, tactfully send your "feelers" or "antennas" out. You can learn a lot by *sensing things out* through informal channels. Better strategic positioning can result from knowledge through the "grapevine."

- *Socialize:* No one can operate as an island and be totally successful. Networking begins at your work environment. As a nurse-manager, be visible at your organization's social events. The non-threatening and relaxed atmosphere offers opportunity for informal social interaction and networking. It is a welcome relief from the stress of running your unit or department, and may even enable you to pick up valuable information through the grapevine.

Finally, be aware that it is important in general to tune in cautiously. Know when to *button* your lip, and *think* before you *speak.* Squelch rumors, and never let your boss learn from the informal network what he/she should have heard first from you. Politics is not a *dirty* word; it is simply a word that has been *dirtied* by the actions of people.

Do not generate *smoke without fire.* Remember, organizational politics does not end with being a *glamorous salesperson.* It is much more important that you combine being politically savvy with producing results. The bottom-line of effective organizational politics is *productivity*, not *popularity.* The former stands the test of time; the latter fades when *"cheerleaders"* are gone.

CHAPTER 6
EFFECTIVE COMMUNICATION

What is communication?

Communication is the verbal or non-verbal interaction between individuals or groups, and is commonly aimed at informing, explaining, instructing, and inspiring for the purpose of accomplishing a desired outcome. It is the formal or informal process of exchanging information and/or ideas from one source (the sender) to another (the receiver). Communication is formal when it is written in the form of books, letters, memos, bulletin, notices, and posters, or when presented in slides, audio or video format. It can also be informal—nonverbal such as by signs, body language, gestures, clothing, space and even time. Some aspects of verbal communication may be informal depending on the context and/or audience, as in impromptu speech or during a conversation. Nonverbal communication is as important as verbal communication because the intended message can also be distorted or misunderstood. A great many people are unaware of the nonverbal messages they give or receive.

Workplace communication is critically important because it affects organizational outcomes positively or negatively. Besides person-to-person communication, cross-functional communication (across and between functions) has become a staple in modern organizations.

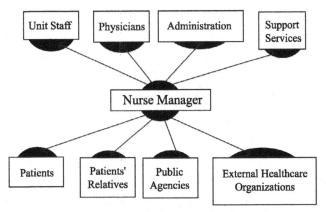

Figure 6: Nurse-Manager's typical communication web

Common Problems

The American workforce is now made up of diverse groups of people from all parts of the world, with workers and patients forming a microcosm of this population. A manager must, therefore, make the effort to reach out and interact with his/her constituents. It is not uncommon to hear some people refer to others as having a *communication problem.* Being born in an English-speaking society or having a college education does not guarantee that someone will not have a communication problem. Regardless of demographic characteristics, communication is most effective when both sender and receiver of a message understand the message's purpose and meaning, and respond accordingly. Writing and verbal (including presentation) communication skills are very critical to professional management success. Regular reading will be helpful in honing conventional communication and interpersonal skills.

Basic day-to-day communication problems may arise due to a number of other reasons such as:

- *Technical deficiency* (lack of understanding of the written and verbal components of the language in use, or ignorance of the discipline being communicated about).

- *Semantic discrepancy* (differences in perceived meaning or individual interpretation between sender and receiver).

- *Ethno-centricism* (disrespect or disregard of the other person's cultural background, or a feeling of superiority of one's own culture).

- *Eclectic confusion* (arising from inability to synthesize information from multiple sources).

- *Content ambiguity* (absence or lack of clarity, or a distorted frame of reference).

Communication problems can arise at any time or point in the communication process.

Some patients are known to file complaints or even sue for *emotional distress* because of their perception that a nurse "gave me an uncomfortable look." Effective communication is especially important in the healthcare industry where wrong interpretations of messages may mean the difference between life and death. It is critical, therefore, that what we communicate is exactly received and interpreted as we intended, as any deviation may affect patient care outcome.

Another aspect of communication is the way we come across to our audience. We may be perceived as aggressive or assertive. Many people confuse the two, thus exhibiting flawed communication. Being assertive allows you to communicate your feelings without appearing threatening. Most people will work and relate with truly assertive people. On the other hand, being aggressive makes you appear threatening to your audience, even though your communication may not be so intended. Most people are usually uncomfortable in such situations. As an aspiring manager, you will need to acquire assertiveness skills. This can be accomplished by attending formal workshops/seminars on the topic, practicing at every opportunity, and observing those whose assertive communication style you admire. Numerous audio and video tapes on the market can also be helpful.

Some Effective Communication Tips

- Think clearly before writing or speaking; some experts advise that you *listen to yourself.* Thinking clearly also involves having in-depth knowledge of the subject in question.

- Make it simple—whether formal or informal. Without sacrificing tact, write or speak to the point, and avoid *parables.* It makes it easier for your audience to decode.

- Keep an open mind. Open communication allows for the free flow of information in an environment of candor, fairness, and respect. However, be careful that your *openness* does not become an invitation to chaos and confusion. If unchecked, it can become clogged with "undesirable messages and *jamming signals!*

- Listen carefully, and avoid unwarranted interruptions; be patient.

- Reinforce the speaker through positive body language that indicates your interest.

- Avoid critical language, negatives and absolutes. Do not indulge in the *blame game.*

CHAPTER 7
ETHICS

*Always do what is right. It will gratify most of the people,
and astound the rest*
  *--Mark Twain from an address to the Young People's Society,
Greenpoint Presbyterian Church, Brooklyn, New York, February
16, 1901*

*Service above Self—He profits most who serves best. The
four-way test: Of the things we think, say or do:
Is it THE TRUTH? Is it FAIR to all concerned? Will
it build GOODWILL and BETTER FRIENDSHIPS?
Will it be BENEFICIAL to ALL CONCERNED?*
  --Rotary International

Overview

In discussing ethics, some people hold the view that ethics
is not discipline-specific. In other words, there simply is
ethics notwithstanding the discipline being discussed.
This further presumes that there is no right reason for doing
the wrong thing. Situational or contingency ethicists would
disagree. Nonetheless, we will explore some basics, especially
as they relate to nursing ethics.

In approaching the subject, it is important to understand
some fundamental facts such as the definition of ethics,
determinants of ethical standards, practices, behavior,

dilemma, and the concept of social responsibility. Ethics are moral standards that guide behavior or conduct. Thus, these standards regulate moral judgments relating to issues of right and wrong, good and bad. While *morality* deals with fundamental principles that shape character, *values* are enduring ideals or beliefs that lend meaning to one's purpose in life. Values provide the framework that propel human behavior at specific points in someone's life, and are often guided by a *Code of Ethics* or list of standards intended to influence personal and professional conduct.

Values may change over time due to intrinsic or extrinsic experiences. For example, one's ethnocentric values may be altered over time due to diversity or sensitivity training or association with a person of opposite ethnicity. However, truths and principles remain unaffected by changes in time or human experiences. While the limitations of this text will not allow for detailed treatment of the subject of ethics, we will briefly look at how moral philosophy identifies two overarching concepts—deontology and utilitarianism.

Deontological ethics is a super-ordinate concept similar to Lawrence Kohlberg's post-conventional level of morality whereby right must be pursued regardless of, and who is affected by, the consequences. Deontology is the *golden rule* of ethics—treating others the way you would like to be treated. It would require, for instance, that you tell your patient the truth about their condition, because you would expect the same if the position was reversed. It also examines motives for right or wrong behavior.

Utilitarianism justifies the goodness of an action if that action benefits the greatest number of people. Thus your moral obligation as a manager is to pursue actions and/or decisions that will benefit the largest segment of your stakeholders.

You must watch out for situations where deontological and utilitarian ethics conflict, as such situations will present the most ethical dilemmas. For example, if you do not believe in *euthanasia,* would you administer a lethal dose to a terminally ill patient whose advance directives and the desire of his/her surviving relatives are in favor of *euthanasia.* If you stick to your beliefs, you satisfy the condition of doing unto others as you would want done onto you; but you will have violated utilitarianism—the greatest *good* for the greatest number (the patient and the patient's relatives)!

Ethical Dilemmas

An ethical dilemma, like the one just described, arises when there is conflict between one's ethical beliefs/personal objectives and obligations to prescribed or accepted standards of organizational behavior. Some typical ethical dilemmas in healthcare range from administering euthanasia (the right to die), use of medical marijuana for the terminally ill, patient privacy and confidentiality, organ donation/transplant or use of non-human organs, invitro-fertilization, genetic cloning, cryogenics, pro-life versus pro-choice, use of condoms versus abstinence, prescribing and dispensing the "morning-after" pill, using embryos in stem cell research, to allowing family members' presence during a code. Another ethical dilemma that has faced many medical schools is whether to allow medical students to examine patients, especially women, under anesthesia without the women's permission. Privacy rights questions can also be tough. A renowned athlete was compelled in 1992 to reveal infection with HIV/AIDS after a news magazine was about to go public with the information.

As healthcare workers, our personal disposition toward social issues (such as abortion and alternative life-styles, etc.) may affect our willingness to render care. Some healthcare providers have been disciplined for refusing to compromise their ethical/moral beliefs. In 1996, a K-mart pharmacist lost her job for refusing "to fill Birth control prescriptions on moral or religious grounds." A local pharmacist in Fort Worth, Texas, once told a patient "I personally don't believe in birth control and therefore I'm not going to fill your prescription." A Milwaukee family physician does not prescribe the pill to her patients. According to Sarah Sturmon Dale, "laws are vague on the subject. But two states, South Dakota and Arkansas, have passed laws that explicitly protect pharmacists who refuse to fill birth-control prescriptions on moral or religious grounds." Personal integrity, objectivity related to nursing notes, and misconduct among co-workers (e.g. substance abuse, and other organizational malpractices) are also issues that the nurse-manager would deal with.

Ethical dilemmas may also involve decisions and/or choices that are perceived as ethical but illegal, or legal but unethical. The matrix below illustrates the relationship between law and ethics.

Yes	Lack of legal compliance	Ethical Management
Is it ethical?	Illegal & Unethical	Lack of Ethics
No		

| | No | **Is It Legal?** | Yes |

Figure 7: Legal/Ethical management matrix

Source: *Exploring the World of Business, Blanchard, Schewe, Nelson, Hiam; Worth Publishers, 1996, p.102*

Managers must be aware that their decisions and actions will constantly come under ethical scrutiny, and that their motivations will be questioned. As a manager you must, therefore, be ready to defend such actions or decisions justifying your motivations. Dilemmas usually have no absolute, clear cut, solutions. When faced with unsettling ethical dilemmas, explore ways of resolving them including the following:

- Obtain, consider, and assess all the facts

- Identify all stakeholders

- Determine any and all legal and/or ethical concerns or implications

- Identify how your personal morality aligns with conventional ethical frameworks

- Follow the established written policies of your organization

- Consult others in the organization (superiors, peers, unaffected subordinates) and determine if a precedent exists, and if such precedent conforms to your organization's code of ethics, is legal and/or defensible common practice in the organization.

- Develop and prioritize an action plan (with alternative courses of action)

- Determine the legality, probability of success and cost implications of a chosen course of action, and if such action can survive rigorous external scrutiny and be replicated in other decision settings.

Elements of Ethical Standards and Practices

Some Management and Ethics theorists believe that ethical *standards* and *practices* are generally influenced by four major elements (legality, common practice, code of ethics, and personal ethics). *Legality* compels adherence to national laws and enactments whether they are ethical or unethical. *Common practice,* whether neutral or sectarian, legal or illegal, ethical or unethical, results from organization-wide or industry-wide practices, and may be litigated or prosecuted when exposed.

Code of ethics persuades managers to act in consonance with desirable practices dictated by the manager's profession or enshrined in the organization's mission statement(s). *Personal ethics* may be **moral** (dictated by a manager's voluntary submission to a code of ethics or to the highest moral convictions), **amoral** (morally neutral*);* and **immoral** (ethical aberration).

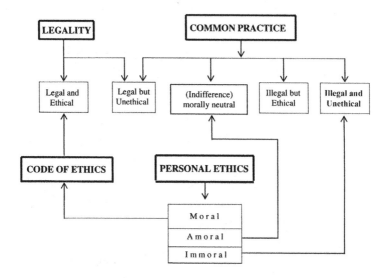

Figure 8: Elements of Ethical Standards and Practices

Ethical behavior can be influenced by factors within the organization, the individual, and outside the organization.

Factors within the Organization

- Policies, rules and regulations emanating from the mission statement, code of ethics and management philosophy.

- Unwritten activities and practices (good or bad) that go on.

- Nature of top management leadership.

- Organizational pressures to increase and improve productivity.

- Organizational resources.

- Reward structure or Reinforcement systems.

Individual Factors

- Personal upbringing.

- Value systems developed through religious, school, and other social interactions

- Needs for personal and professional growth.

- Family and other domestic responsibilities.

- Age and personal ego.

- Tenure with the organization.

Factors outside the organization

- Professional codes of ethics.
- Surveillance by moderating influences (media, interest groups, etc.)
- Laws, regulations and regulatory agencies.
- Ethical mood in the external environment—political, economic, social and cultural
- Severity of consequence for ethical and moral breaches
- Competition

While nurse-managers should remain cognizant of health care ethics, they must become adept at dealing with management-related ethical situations that become part of their work routine. Examples of such situations would be pressure to cut corners in response to tight budgets that may adversely impact patient care, or when a subordinate alters documentation to conceal negligent behavior. In order to minimize ethical dilemmas, the nurse-manager must, *a priori,* set standards of ethical conduct for his/her subordinates— standards that he/she must also be willing to be judged by.

Social Responsibility

Social responsibility is an organization's obligation to seek both the welfare of its internal stakeholders and that of society as a whole. Management theorists stress three major views of social responsibility—the classical view, the accountability view, and the public view. The *classical view* holds that an organization exists to create profit and wealth for its investors through the orderly production and marketing of goods, services and ideas. Any deviation from this objective violates the fundamental tenets of the free enterprise system. By creating wealth, organizations provide jobs, expand the tax base, provide choice, and energize the economy.

The *accountability view* suggests that an organization balance its commitment to investors with a concern for the needs and well-being of society. Its employees should likewise actively participate in their respective communities.

The *public view* takes the extreme position that organizations should have the primary goal of acting as social catalysts to influence public policy for the common good. For-profit-organizations must be duty-bound to help eradicate poverty, provide housing and check urban decay, fight crime, and eliminate hunger.

Social Impact

Our society continues to experience technical, social and legal changes that act as catalysts in modifying human and organizational behavior. These changes further heighten public awareness and expectations of moral and ethical performance by professionals in every field of human endeavor. Whether it is in politics, business, religion, medicine, nursing or other social frontiers, important socio-economic and political issues have given ethics a new stature of importance and relevance.

Social issues such as drugs, alcohol, abortion, sexual/lifestyle orientation, environmental protection, violence in the work place, guns, and gun control will continue to shape the way organizations relate to various stakeholders. There is no doubt that both the medical and nursing professions will continue to wrestle with these and many other ethical and moral issues that affect their practice.

CHAPTER 8
THE HUMAN ELEMENT

Human Nature

The human element is perhaps one of the most challenging aspects of a manager's job. Human beings are the single most unpredictable element in organizations. People, unlike machines, have different personalities and individual goals, prefer different things, have opposing lifestyles, come from different backgrounds, and are indeed as diverse as can be—gender, ethnicity, thought processes, and other extrinsic and intrinsic characteristics. Employees consciously or unconsciously bring their *baggage* from home to work. People problems may take more than fifty percent of your time as a manager and sap your energy and sanity on a continuing basis. Blending your clinical/technical skills with some sense of humor, and a generous dose of good interpersonal relations is vital to your success as a nurse-manager.

Conflict

One aspect of the human element that will test your leadership and managerial skills to the limit is conflict. Conflict in work situations is inescapable. It is often fueled by the desire for leverage, the struggle for power and control (domination), the competition for limited resources, and sometimes the sheer indulgence in a war of wits or elevation of one's personal ego. According to Cyril Soffer (1972), conflict is a game "in which the aims of the conflicting parties are not only to gain the desired values but also to neutralize, injure or eliminate their rivals."[3] Conflict may also result from unanticipated change, especially when such change is perceived as a threat to an established domain of comfort. Other causes of conflict in the work place include prejudice, poor communication and aggressiveness.

Types of Conflict

Game theorists have identified two major types of conflicts: zero-sum and nonzero sum. Zero-sum situations are strictly competitive ones in which the parties involved have exactly contrary preferences. In such situations every gain for one contestant yields a corresponding loss for the other, e.g. a football game. Offensive strategies are counteracted or nullified by defensive or preemptive strategies. Zero-sum conflicts destroy organizational *health and cohesion,* hence they are sometimes referred to as dysfunctional. Non-zero sum conflicts are preferable because there is no strict competition or desire for territory. In such a situation, there is at least one outcome for which the preferences of the players are not strictly opposed—e.g. the goal of a health care team is to ensure the patient's recovery from illness. By its nature, nonzero-sum conflict at least permits limited cooperation between opposing parties. Because nonzero sum conflicts further the cause of organizations, they are regarded as functional.

In work relationships, vertical and horizontal conflicts also occur. Vertical conflict exists when there are differences between superiors and subordinates. Horizontal conflict involves domains of practice, expertise, autonomy and authority, often existing between departments or individuals at the same level.

Reactions to Conflict

Whatever the cause, nature and type of conflict, the basic fact is that if one person or group perceives that they are having a conflict with another, conflict then exists. Leaders in organizations are constantly faced with conflict with employees and conflict among employees. Conflict in the work place needs to be approached constructively to prevent negative results.

Usually, the strategy should be to resolve or reduce the incidence of conflict in organizations. In doing so, it is important to understand that groups or individuals react differently to conflict. Groups tend to react by becoming more cohesive, especially if individual members believe that their collective or corporate self-interest and survival depend on the group's own survival. Individuals who stay to fight may do so out of a natural instinct for self-preservation or out of sheer anxiety. On the other hand, individuals may choose flight. Highly charged anxiety can breed emotional discomfort, lack of concentration and can even create unsatisfying coping mechanisms like denial, escapism or aggression.

Conflict Resolution

Conflict can be resolved either peacefully or by the use of force. Effective conflict management and resolution must deal with the cause of conflict, rather than applying *band-aid* solutions to the symptoms. It is a grand illusion to think that the conflict *will just go away*. We offer the following strategies:

- Confront the source or cause of the conflict in an honest, professional and truthful manner. Identifying the source or cause of the conflict is a major breakthrough in arriving at a solution. For example, conflict brought about by role ambiguity could simply be resolved through role clarification by referring to the job description, developing a role matrix and re-educating or re-orienting parties to what their roles are. Hierarchy-based conflicts can be resolved through redesign of the organizational structure showing clear delineation of authority.

- Deal with the conflict promptly. Do not wait until it goes from a minor incident to a major crisis.

- Attack the conflict, not the individual or individuals concerned.

- If emotions are high, allow for a *cooling off period*. Where feasible, interpersonal conflicts may be resolved by reducing to a minimum interaction between the individuals concerned; for example, posting them to different units.

- Emphasize super-ordinate goals, especially if individuals or groups involved are going to be interacting continuously over time. Help the group or individual choose a goal on which everyone can agree, and thus divert their attention and energies to a more productive endeavor.

- Encourage compromise and consensus; but do it in such a way as to blur any appearance of leverage or condescension in favor of one party over another.

- Depending on the nature of the conflict, refer to previous solutions to conflicts of a similar nature. For consistency, identify established organizational policies and procedures that may address or apply to such a conflict.

- Be objective, fair and impartial so that your decision/ solution is able to withstand scrutiny, and restore faith of the offended party.

- Establish guidelines and deadlines for implementing conflict resolution decisions, and provide immediate feedback to all parties.

- If necessary, encourage the warring parties to attend conflict resolution workshops

- Seek the advice of top management or use the services of your organization's employee assistance program.

Since you as a manager will set the tone for conflict management, you should endeavor to be:
- *Innovative* (seek new ways to improve operations and to resolve conflicts)

- *Respectful* of authority, subordinates, and other personnel

- *Inspiring* (be someone your subordinates can proudly look up to).

- *Have* a high sense of emotional maturity.

Employee Development

In order for your employees to be effective, you should embark on a program of continuously developing them. A critical step in this task is to identify, attract, and hire the best employees in the first place. You will need to rely immensely on your interviewing and perceptive skills. During orientation on your employee's first day on the job, clarify your goals and expectations. Let them know what you are about and how they are expected to fit into the whole picture. Provide a detailed orientation (preferably using a checklist approach) as most employees become disillusioned on their first day on the job due to poor orientation.

As your employees mature on their jobs, seek ways to encourage their personal and professional growth and development. Outside seminars, workshops, and conferences can also be complemented with unit-level in-house in-services. You can accomplish this by identifying and using available expertise within your organization. Save cost and logistics headaches by combining training resources with similar organizations within your area, or by periodically contracting with *affordable external* consultants. The impact of technology on training can be tremendous in a modern organization; explore the many options available. Encourage your employees to undertake a personal skills inventory from time to time so as to identify areas that they need improvement.

Motivating Employees

In terms of motivation, make a conscious effort to identify what makes your employees *"tick."* Different things motivate different people. To some, it may be money while to others it may be a challenging and happy work environment, clear goals/expectations, availability of the proper work tools, or the ability to have a say in decisions that affect their work. Experience shows that people can go the extra mile if they feel valued, appreciated, and paid what they are worth. A genuine praise or comment for a job well done is a powerful motivator, especially after a very demanding task. Being honest encourages employees to be committed and willing to work toward improvement. To this end, it may be desirable to establish monthly or biweekly meetings to discuss operational matters. Also, do not hesitate to convene *emergency* meetings if the occasion demands. Your employees want to know that you are willing to tackle their problems without resorting to needless bureaucracy. You must lead by example, striving at all times to represent in both concept and practice that type of leader you want your employees to emulate.

You can give people a sense of value by:

- Demonstrating genuine interest and concern about how they feel—occasionally ask your employees how their work is and be sure to *listen*. Otherwise, you may appear insincere or merely *fronting*.

- Building pride, status, and identification in your team—makes your team feel that they can be counted upon for their support and expertise.

- Rewarding outstanding accomplishments promptly and commensurately.

- Being receptive and supportive of ideas and suggestions that will improve any aspect of your operations and accord appropriate recognition to the originator of such ideas—let your employees *shine* in their own *deserving spotlight*.

- Sharing relevant information with your team and seeking their input.

- Giving employees immediate feedback as to how *specifically* their inputs solved an organizational problem.

In general, you must be consistent in handling employee issues, because any element of inconsistency (real or perceived) breeds distrust.

It is vital that you provide the right type of leadership. If any team member is not *playing* well, it is your responsibility to identify the reasons for such deficiency, and initiate a corrective plan. You should see your unit/department as a *learning organization*—one in which employees are encouraged/challenged to identify problems and suggest solutions in a dynamic work atmosphere, thus fostering *intrapreneurship* and ensuring organizational growth, competitiveness and survival. Richard L. Daft, an organization theory expert, states that "... new organizations are knowledge-based, which means they are designed to handle ideas and information, with each employee becoming an expert in one or several conceptual tasks."[4]

Diversity

The face of the US workforce is constantly changing. The nursing profession now includes more male members than in the past. Because of economic pressures, we also see the elderly returning to or staying longer in the work force. There are also employees with varying lifestyle preferences. The nursing shortage a few years ago forced many institutions to recruit nurses from other countries, leading to a massive influx of people with different languages, cultural backgrounds and practice experiences. The customer/client/patient mix is also changing. While these trends will continue to be a challenge to native, *homegrown,* US nurse-managers, it will be more so for those managers who choose to remain ethnocentric, and less so for those who are open-minded and receptive to the best employees regardless of their ethnicity, national origin, creed and/or other demographic persuasions. When excellent individuals who do not fit our traditional preference are *"locked out,"* we all as a society lose the benefits of their expertise.

One misconception about diversity is that it is supposed to change you. Yes and no. Yes, because it will make you more sensitive and appreciative of the good in the differences in others, and thus promote *understanding*, and not necessarily *acceptance.* For instance, as a result of understanding someone's cultural background relating to eating with chop-sticks, you may be willing to share the same dining table with them even if you do not accept the practice of eating with chop-sticks because you understand it is not intended to compromise or re-wire your core individuality. You remain fundamentally who you are.

Remember, the strength of your unit or department may yet lie in its diversity. One bumper sticker expression says that "minds are like parachutes, they work better when open." As a nurse-manager, your behavior toward diverse employees or patients sends a clear message of tolerance or intolerance and where you stand. You owe it to *all* your employees and to your diverse customer groups to be fair, just, and impartial. Simply put, treat them the way you would like to be treated.

In summary, you can deal with stereotyping and prejudices in any or combination of the following ways:

- Train and develop your employees periodically to understand the positive influence of diversity in your organization, emphasizing the common goals of your organization.

- "Walk the talk" by setting the right example in your own interpersonal relationships inside and outside your organization.

- Be firm in your intolerance of stereotyping and prejudice. This must include the non-tolerance of inflammatory and derogatory language, verbal or nonverbal.

- Make group job assignments as diverse as possible along ethno-cultural, racial and gender lines.

- When problems arise, confront them honestly and candidly. Use such incidents as an educational opportunity.

- Be patient with your employees. Remember age-old practices do not disappear "overnight."

Your goal should be to look for and build on the strengths of each employee, while you also devise ways to assist them out of their deficiencies. Finally, remember as a manager the light is *turned* on you, and you must be tolerant of others who differ from you in many respects. Experience shows that differences in human relationships tend to blur as we all consciously seek out those qualities that enable us to blend our capabilities and ascend to common and higher ground.

CHAPTER 9
PROFESSIONALISM, NURSING IMAGE AND CAREER OPTIONS

Woes of the Profession

As was pointed out earlier, nursing over the years has not been accorded appropriate recognition as a respectable profession. The relics of this notion, regrettably, are still very much alive. In our society, many other disciplines such as teaching, law, medicine and engineering have no problem being accorded respect and recognition as professions. It is equally fashionable and common to refer to athletes as being in professional sports. Like these and many other professions, the discipline of professional nursing requires years of education involving academic and intellectual rigor in addition to skills development through clinicals and internships. In some cases, further training is undertaken to acquire specialized skills. The practice of nursing itself bears immensely on the demonstration of not only superior skill and judgment, but the tactful application of all human senses.

Entry into professional nursing practice is preceded by passing a prescribed Board (licensure) examination.

Thereafter, continuous professional development is undertaken in order to remain certified or credentialed.

While nursing requires the application of scientific knowledge, it is also one of the most demanding of all forms of human *art*. Nurses in both academia and industry have collaborated amongst themselves and with other professionals to carry out rigorous research, thus contributing to a body of knowledge that either reduces human suffering or improves its health and well-being.

Improving Nursing's Professional Image

How can the image of nursing as a profession be improved? From the point of view of a professional nurse, a number of things come to mind:

- *Sound Knowledge*—you cannot claim to be a professional without having sound knowledge of your field.

- *Professionalism*—*your* grooming, your taste, your outlook—all have to exude quality and a touch of class.

- *Ability to communicate effectively*—the importance of oral and written communication cannot be over-emphasized.

- A *positive attitude*—many people fail because of their negative attitude. Control the environment; don't let it control you.

- *Community Involvement/Networking*—this will enhance your visibility in a positive light. Network with nursing as well as other non-nursing organizations that share the ideals of your profession. Even if non-nursing organizations do not share your ideals, get involved and strive to understand theirs in order to enrich or persuade them toward yours.

Enhancing both a personal and a professional image does not necessarily mean compromising your principles or ideals; it does not mean trying to be what you are not, neither is it misrepresenting the tenets of the profession. Rather, it is the concerted effort of *flowering and fruiting* the best in you and your profession, and genuinely *marketing* it for the benefit of all who are, and ultimately will be, associated with your experience and expertise.

Read, explore, research and participate in other scholarly activities to reinvigorate your intellect and to contribute to the long-term survival of your discipline, its acceptance and recognition. One sure way to degrade your profession and guarantee its demise is to shy away from the pursuit of new knowledge. Challenge new frontiers of knowledge. For example, nursing like all other disciplines, must keep pace with technology—whether it is in terms of new products or new processes that will enhance patient therapy and restore health. We should continue to update our knowledge of computers, and developments in biomedical technology. Just as technology has revolutionized teaching with computer-assisted instruction/ distance learning, and manufacturing with computer-aided design and computer-aided manufacturing, healthcare has also been considerably impacted by computers and technology— from diagnostics to the management of patient database.

The sheer volume of patient traffic and the need to integrate administrative and clinical data, as well as the need to accelerate work protocols, monitor resource utilization, develop patient education, enhance pharmacy performance, handle tons of billing, and reduce the amount of paper work, etc.

make investment in automation very worthwhile. Real-time information sharing has been enhanced through connection to vast networks and organizational intranets, thus accelerating data access, ensuring more accurate diagnoses, and improving patient care outcomes.

Let us leave you with the following ten tips from Donna Sollenberger, former President of Patient Care Services at MD Anderson Health Center, Houston, Texas, during her presentation to the University of Texas System Committee on the Advancement of Women and Minorities (1996). When asked what had helped her professionally along the way, she urged participants to:

1. Work hard, set good examples as you never know who's watching or depending on you.

2. Attend to details, but also be able to look at the larger picture

3. Don't say you can't do something; think of problem-solving as circular not linear.

4. Be tactful, but honest and always direct; deliver even difficult messages with compassion.

5. Believe everybody's contribution is valuable, no matter how small

6. Maintain a good sense of humor and smile a lot—keeps your audience relaxed.

7. Don't forget to promote yourself and your abilities without bragging.

8. Be doggedly determined to succeed.

9. Don't be afraid to make mistakes.

10. Be optimistic.

In concluding her remarks, she said that "credibility is earned, not anointed; don't be afraid of hiring talented people, give them freedom, develop professional relationships built on respect and equality."

Career Options

While many nurses derive joy in doing hands-on patient care, it is also true that they experience burnout very rapidly. Fortunately, some changes in the modern work place have given rise to more career options for nurses. Some of these options are as:

Advanced Practice Nurses:
> Nurse Practitioners
> Nurse Anesthetists
> Clinical Nurse Specialists
> Nurse Midwives

Administrators:
> Hospital Administrator
> Vice President or Director of Patient Services
> Vice President for Clinic Administration
> Chief Nursing Officer
> Director of Community Health Services
> Director of Nursing
> Home Health Administrator

Quality Assurance Manager
Case Manager
Nurse Recruiter
Nurse Attorney or Certified Legal Nurse Consultant

Nurse entrepreneurs are also breaking new grounds

by establishing their own businesses or partnering with other nurses or healthcare professionals. This group is usually made up of clinicians with specialized knowledge, practice, and/or experience who find a niche and capitalize on it. Typical examples can be found in the areas of research, continuing education for nurses, consulting (including legal), grant writing, publishing, lobbying, and risk management.

A word of caution – whatever you choose to do, make sure that it is something you will enjoy—something you already have a passion for, or are willing and able to master with some mentoring or nurturing. Proceed cautiously; identify those who may already be in the field, get as much information as you can, and join relevant professional associations. You cannot network enough!

CHAPTER 10
ACCOUNTING AND BUDGETING BASICS
Accounting and Financial Management

The information in this chapter is not intended to turn you into a sudden financial wizard, but rather to help clear some of the maze in the often confusing and murky language of business. You are encouraged to take some basic accounting and related business courses and to attend, whenever possible, workshops offered on the subject.

As managers in the new atmosphere of healthcare management, nurse managers will find it helpful to familiarize themselves with accounting and financial management concepts. While your focus remains top quality patient care, you cannot ignore the business component of your responsibilities.

As healthcare organizations streamline their operations, the need to become financially and administratively competent is no longer an option, but a necessity, especially as nurse managers are being required to shoulder most of their unit's business-related functions such as managing physical, human, and financial resources. Financial information is vital in decision-making at all levels. "The information needs of users are the basis for the three objectives of financial reporting established by the Financial Accounting Standards Board (FASB):"

- To furnish information that is useful in making investment and credit decisions.

- To provide information useful in assessing cash flow prospects

- To provide information about business resources, claims to those resources, and changes in them.[5]

Some Accounting Basics

To some extent, we all make daily decisions in our individual homes that border on accounting and budgeting. Although we are not required by anyone to keep books for running our homes, it makes good financial sense to know what your income is and how much of that income you can spend or save. In business operations, accounting and budgeting are important managerial tools. Accounting involves accumulating, recording, summarizing, reporting, analyzing, and interpreting financial information resulting from business operations. Proper accounting records enable us to determine if our operations are profitable or unprofitable, or if funds received are expended for their designated purposes.

The various branches of accounting include financial accounting, management (or managerial) accounting, auditing, and tax accounting. *Financial accounting* information is generated from day-to-day business transactions of an organization. It caters to the needs of external users who are concerned about the organization's performance in terms of profitability and solvency. These external users include vendors/suppliers, investors, lenders, regulatory agencies, and the general public.

Managerial accounting synthesizes financial information for use by internal managers for planning and decision making. Issues such as costs of providing care, clinical support services, unit or departmental budgets, staffing ratios, and strategies to reduce waste, all fall under managerial accounting.

Auditing is concerned with reviewing and evaluating financial accounting functions to ascertain whether or not appropriate processes and procedures have been followed in recording and reporting financial transactions in accordance with generally accepted accounting principles (GAAP). Some organizations have internal auditors as employees to provide on-going oversight on internal financial and operational controls. There are also external auditors who are not employees of an organization, but conduct independent audits of the financial activities of their client organizations.

Tax accounting deals with an organization's concerns as they relate to identifying tax strategies, implementing tax policies, preparing and filing tax returns, and reviewing ever changing tax laws. The whole idea is for the organization to maximize its tax benefits as it seeks to meet legal tax mandates.

Assets, Liabilities and Capital

Regardless of the type of business, three elements of the accounting equation *(assets = liabilities + capital)* provide the basis for business existence and record keeping. Indeed the accounting equation is a statement of the balance sheet. Assets represent the things that a business owns to help it carry out its normal operations, "the essence of which is expected future benefits" (Needles, Powers, Crosson, 2005). Assets may be classified as current *(liquid or circulating)* or long term *(fixed or strategic)*. Current assets usually have a short life-span of one year or less. Examples are cash, medical and office supplies inventory, pre-paids, short-term notes, and accounts receivable. Long-term assets last longer—anywhere from two to over twenty years. They are used in the continuous generation of organizational wealth, and are depreciated over time.

Depreciation is the systematic depletion in value and cost of a tangible asset over its estimated useful life. Examples are buildings, plants, machinery, medical equipment such as x-ray machines, operating room equipment, cardiac monitors, stretchers, beds, and office equipment. Depreciation is a non-cash expense which reduces an organization's tax liability by reducing its taxable income.

Liabilities represent an organization's financial obligations. They may also be current or long-term. An example of a current liability is a debt due to be paid within one year, such as cost of medical supplies or short-term notes and accounts payable. An example of a long-term liability is a 20-year mortgage note on a building facility or a five-year bank loan for financing the purchase of a piece of medical equipment. Capital (also known as *owners' equity*) is the amount invested in a business. It is usually expressed as the difference between assets and liabilities. Two major sources of capital are debt and/or equity. Debt is capital from borrowing or leverage. Equity is capital from personal or non-debt sources The typical capital section of a balance sheet encompasses shareholders' equity and retained (or undistributed) earnings.

HEALWELL HOSPITAL
Balance Sheet
At December 31, 2XXX

Current Assets:

Cash	$500,000		
Medical Supplies Inventory	$100,000		
Total Current Assets			$ 600,000

Long-term Assets:

X-ray equipment	$1,000,000		
Less Accumulated Depreciation	$ 200,000	$ 800,000	
Buildings	$2,000,000		
Less Accumulated Depreciation	$ 100,000	$1,900,000	
Total long-term assets			$2,700,000
Total Assets			$3,300,000

Current Liabilities:

Accounts Payable	$ 10,000	

Long-term Liabilities:

Mortgage Payable	$1,800,000	
Total Liabilities		$1,810,000

Capital:

Capital	$1,000,000	
Retained Earnings	$ 190,000	$1,490,000
Total Liabilities and Capital:		$3,300,000

Figure 9: Hypothetical Balance Sheet

The balance sheet, as already stated, is a statement of an organization's assets, liabilities and capital at a specific point in time, usually the last day of a month or year. Total assets should normally equal the sum of liabilities and capital.

Another important accounting or financial statement is the income statement. It is sometimes referred to as the operating statement or profit/loss statement. It essentially summarizes the revenues and expenses for a specific period of time, usually a year. If total revenues exceed total expenses, there is profit; if the reverse is the case, then there is loss. Traditionally organizations carry out their activities with money derived from sale of their products, services, or ideas. This money is called revenue. In the process of such activities, organizations also spend money or generate debt. The money so spent is referred to as expense(s) or, in conventional budgetary language, expenditures. In a healthcare organization, patient volume is a very important factor that drives revenue; however, your major challenge as a clinic manager is to keep costs low without compromising patient care.

A simplified income statement is shown below:

HEALWELL HOSPITAL

Income Statement for Year Ended December 31, 2XXX

Revenue		$2,000,000
Less:		
Cost of Services	$1,200,000	
Other expenses	$ 100,000	
Total expenses		$1,300,000
Profit before taxes		$ 700,000
Tax 30% (*if applicable)*		$ 210,000
Net Profit		$ 490,000

Figure 10: Hypothetical Income Statement

Budgets and Budgeting

A budget is a plan or forecast of operations expressed in financial terms. Budgeting is a rigorous process that activates plans, and is subject to extensive and elaborate management deliberations. A budget is the ultimate outcome of a process of gathering, organizing and articulating data into an action document. It sets forth the vision, charts the course and cost of fulfilling the vision, and identifies the expected or desirable outcomes if everything goes according to plan. Remember, because a budget is a plan, specific outcomes/results are expected. Sometimes those outcomes materialize as planned; sometimes, they do not. A manager must, therefore, analyze outcomes to determine any variance(s), favorable or unfavorable, and the reasons for the variance(s). To do so, a manager is guided by proper benchmarking, i.e. standards or yardsticks for measuring performance. Because a budget underscores top management's revenue and expenditure expectations, it becomes a tool for resource allocation. There are different types of budgets such as cash budget, capital budget, operating budget, zero-base, program budget, performance budget, and personnel budgets.

A **cash budget** is a forecast of expected cash receipts and payments. Expected cash receipts are usually added to beginning cash balance in order to determine total cash that will be available for carrying out day-to-day operating activities. Cash payment for activities is subtracted from total available cash to arrive at the ending cash balance. Organizations often determine beforehand a *desired end of period cash balance;* if the desired cash balance is less than the actual ending cash, then the organization may raise a short-term loan.

A **capital budget** is a strategic or long-term plan involving expenditures to expand, modernize, replace, acquire, or even abandon certain services, products, equipment, building, and/or facilities. Decisions regarding capital investments are usually influenced by management's desire to reduce costs, increase revenue, improve services or products, preempt the competition, and generally to ensure long-term organizational survival. In the healthcare environment, management may seek to:

- replace dilapidated equipment by introducing state-of-the-art medical equipment for certain specialties or subspecialties

- expand existing services

- introduce new products

- acquire a research organization in order to enhance its cutting-edge position in technology and biomedical research or

- abandon an existing service by outsourcing, selling or outright liquidation.

Capital budget decisions commonly involve multiple persons within an organization, and may take a fairly long time to accomplish because of their strategic consequences. As a nurse manager, your input will be requested by top management from time to time regarding strategic improvements in your particular area of operation. So be ready! A unit's budget is eventually summarized and made part of a comprehensive organizational master (capital) budget.

An **operating budget** emphasizes a profit goal. Because of its short-term nature, managers are faced with the need to specify an income or profit target usually as a rate of return on investment, determine activity volume or level for predetermined revenue and expenses, and later compare actual profit against planned profit. Sometimes operating plans work out as envisioned; sometimes they do not. Any number of variables may be altered to affect future operating outcomes, such as:

- identifying inefficiencies to reduce the cost of services while holding selling price constant;

- reducing price to increase volume of sales

- improving existing product or service quality;

- creating new products or services; and

- ensuring prompt accessibility or availability of products or services to consumers.

An essential element in operating budgets is tight control in order to reach the profit goal.

As a nurse-manager, you may pay particular attention to the area of performance and personnel budget.

Performance budgeting is concerned with the relationship between resource inputs and outcomes in a particular department or unit instead of a program as in program budgeting. Thus, the focus is on the specifics of a task, activity, job, or function. Performance budgeting places an immense burden on unit managers (as cost centers) to justify their budget proposals.

Personnel budgeting is simply the process of identifying the number of people needed to perform an activity or produce a product. It includes the cost of acquiring, training/developing and placing employees on the job. Employees' base pay and benefits, including vacation pay, insurance, sick time and other related factors are also figured in the personnel budget.

Determining staff requirements to meet the needs of a unit is critical in the budget process. The nurse manager needs to be familiar with the calculation of FTE (full time equivalent), a concept commonly used in business. "Accurate calculation of the full time equivalent (FTE) requirements for the unit will help to prevent unnecessary use of PRN and overtime staff..." (Osuagwu 1993). Efficient human resource utilization in a unit means that consideration has been given to work load, shift requirement, and related contingencies. In general, an FTE is required to work 40 hrs/week or 160 hrs/month or 2080 hours/year, assuming no vacations, sick time, holidays, or educational days. However, these must be accounted for or your FTE requirements will not be accurate. Another important consideration in calculating FTE needs is shift length, volume or unit activity as well as complexity/acuity of the patients. Having an 8-hour, 10- hour, or 12-hour shift may make a little difference in your FTE calculation. Both direct and indirect activities related to care should also be accounted for.

It is important to make a contingency allowance to replace staff members who may be absent for one reason or the other. Building this into your budget will allow you to avoid any surprising budget shortfalls, which you may have to explain in a variance report. Budgeting money does not mean that it would be spent; the manager still has the responsibility of ensuring that the most cost-effective approach to staffing is adopted for quality care.

For different reasons, some managers utilize per diem support while others build in extra staff member(s) in their initial budget. Each option has its pros and cons.

The per diem approach does not attract benefits, and offers an appearance of being less costly if the money so budgeted is not utilized. In reality, per diem rates are generally higher when used, and you may end up with a less trained staff from a staffing agency. Per diem nurses do not owe any allegiance to your institution, and may not have any or adequate knowledge about the department or unit, thus, posing more risk in some cases. If you routinely carry the FTE along during the year, you would then expend the related costs in salary and benefits. The choice you make may ultimately depend on the overall financial picture of your institution.

A simple way to build FTE into the budget may be achieved as follows:

1 FTE = 2,080 hours (40 hours/ wk x 52 weeks)

Less *160 hours (vacation, holidays, sick time)

1,920 hours (actual hours worked)

*Hours not worked but paid for, which represents nearly 8% of 1 FTE.

The implication is that you would need to provide for at least 8% of the total FTE requirement in your budget. This should lead to adequate FTE(s) and thus serve as a cushion in your budget, other factors being constant.

Zero-base budgeting (ZBB) challenges and demands that all agency programs be defended. As a matter of fact, ZBB was a spin-off of the ill-fated planning- programming-budgeting system of the late 1960s which was aimed at harmonizing the planning and programming activities of public agencies.

While ZBB eliminates any presumption that the previous year's appropriation will be provided, it demands explanation of achievement relative to previous programs, and justifications for additional resource requirement for existing as well as new activities.

Thus more money cannot simply be allocated blindly to a program without clear and convincing facts and figures. By compelling a unit or department to explore and evaluate alternative ways to achieve objectives or accomplish activities, ZBB provides a thorough analysis of agency programs. The process is "grass roots" based, but is rigorous and involves volumes of paper work that may not be used after all.

Another type of budget is the **program budget**—which is program-based or function-centered. It is concerned with the total cost of a specific program, function, or activity. Usually, specific programs, functions or activities may necessitate cross-functional effort where the ultimate concern is the favorable outcome of the team's efforts; it is not necessarily that of one particular unit or department. A typical example may be an organization- wide campaign to improve employees occupational health and safety. Such a program may involve the following:

Purpose will be to:

- Improve productivity.

- Reduce workplace injuries and thus workmen's compensation cost.

- Reduce sickness-driven absenteeism.

- Enable employees to enjoy an overall sense of physical well-being.

Methodology:

- Enhancing awareness through posters, lectures, video presentations.

- Demonstrating workplace hazards, their consequences and how to avoid them.

- Training on First Aid and CPR (cardio-pulmonary resuscitation).

- Emphasizing balanced meals, exercise and relaxation.

The entire program will involve a cross-section of people from various areas, namely personnel department, information/graphics, physical plant/engineering, occupational medicine staff, nutritionists/dieticians, exercise physiologists, physicians, nurses, and social workers. This program's simplified (typical) budget summary may be as follows:

Program Component	Prior Year Expenditures			Current Year			Proposed Budget
	Budget	Actual	Variance	Budget	Actual	Variance	
Awareness	$20,000	$25,000	($5,000)	$30,000			$40,000
Methods	$30,000	$30,000	$0	$35,000			$45,000
Total	$50,000	$55,000	($5,000)	$65,000			$85,000

Figure 11: Hypothetical Budget Summary

Budget Variances

Like many other instruments of management control, budgets are also affected by inaccurate or insufficient qualitative and quantitative information, and unanticipated or uncontrollable changes in the, legislative, operating, social and economic environments. For example: on July 16, 2004, the news media reported that government was likely to approve obesity as a disease reimbursable by Medicare. Even with the best of estimates and intentions, budgets and actuals may still be discrepant. Variance analysis should be viewed from a corrective and helpful rather than from a punitive perspective. It should be used to explain favorable or unfavorable variances, and not to apportion blame, except of course, if any unfavorable variance was avoidable! As a management tool, it should help an organization improve its budgeting process. For example, causes of favorable variances when identified should be replicated or further improved upon, while unfavorable variances should be analyzed and corrective measures promptly taken.

Budgets provide the benchmark against which outcomes are measured relative to pro-forma standards set over a given period, e.g. projected patient visits versus actual visits, projected admissions versus actual admissions. Both management theorists and practitioners agree that in order for budgets to be an effective managerial tool, budgeted activities must be specific, measurable, attainable, realistic, and time-sensitive. As a control mechanism, budgets can sometimes limit managers' ability to exploit emerging opportunities in a dynamic environment, e.g. inability to effectively meet the needs of a rising patient census due to budgetary restriction or a freeze on hiring PRN help.

Budget Preparation

Organizations traditionally have a budget calendar or budget planning cycle which is simply a sequential and systematic ordering of activities, and which finally results in the official budget. This sequence involves dates for preliminary budget meetings, presentation sessions, drafts, analysis and reviews, hearings (where applicable) final budget preparation, adoption, signing, and dissemination/distribution. At the nurse manager's level, budget preparation is likely to be affected by information such as number of patients, disease acuity levels, supplies and equipment needs, and patient ratio to professional and support personnel. These will, of course, be impacted by the healthcare organization's long-term strategy and objectives.

Factors Influencing Budget Approval

Some important factors that influence budget approval include:

- *Knowledge* of the basic concepts, organizational goals, centrality of the unit and nature of its needs, internal and external economic factors that affect unit operations.

- *Personal operational characteristics of the unit manager:* track record and reputation for integrity, interpersonal skills, ability to be a team player, and a thorough understanding of your organization's mission.

- *Thorough homework:* the manager's ability to produce a document that shows attention to detail—such a document is created by starting on time to gather vital qualitative and quantitative data to support and substantiate budget requests.

- *Professional presentation:* some organizations require the budget's author to make an oral presentation. The manager must exhibit self-confidence, have a thorough command and knowledge of his/her particular department, exhibit the highest standards of professionalism, preempt questions and have ready credible and verifiable answers.

- *Top management or corporate level strategic plans*

Implementing and Monitoring the Budget

Once the budget has been approved and passed on to you, the manager, it becomes your duty to implement and monitor. Monitoring is especially important because of deviations and the need for cost control. You must "watch" or track your budget as well as analyze trends and their effect on your operations. For tracking, you may wish to devise a matrix that shows expense type or sub-head, the variance (difference between budget and actual), and corresponding explanation for the variance.

Once undesirable trends are observed, analyze them and take corrective action promptly. You may want to devise a system of periodic data analysis of selected items that can easily "burst" your budget. For example, note cost changes in telephone calls, supplies, and staff over-time (e.g. watch time cards and compare payouts with actual hours worked). Supplies may run out quickly if your unit suddenly exceeds its budgeted level of patient volume and/or experiences a rise in the level of acute patients. Establish thresholds or benchmarks that will enable you to spot any deviations that may be unnecessarily costing your unit money.

A typical example was when one unit in an organization was *"spending"* three times its average cost for copier services. Monitoring the monthly financial report revealed that another unit was inadvertently using the former's copier identification number/counter! The erring unit had already cost the non-erring unit $1,000 ($500 per month for two months). The error was quickly spotted and corrected because the non-erring unit's manager was alert to, and aware of, her unit's monthly average count for copier usage.

Monitoring can also reveal desirable outcomes such as efficiency (e.g. measured by reduced resource inputs with improved patient care outcome), and effectiveness (e.g. measured by higher rate of patient satisfaction and/or recovery rate following clinical intervention).

Staff Involvement

A critical step in the successful financial management of your unit is staff education and commitment. Note that involvement begets commitment. Involvement will increase not only your employees understanding and knowledge, but also their commitment to stay within the budget. For no apparent strategic reason, some managers have a tendency to treat budgets as "personal" property. Perhaps this affords them a sense of power and control. Do not fall into this trap. Make your employees aware of what has been appropriated within their sphere of operations and services. In this way, they too become partners with you in ensuring that the budget is properly implemented and monitored. Here are some tips on encouraging staff involvement in the budget process:

- Adopt a participatory management style, but insure that participants have been adequately coached/trained, and can contribute meaningfully;

- Do not withhold appropriate information from staff; share information such as variances and the need to avoid unnecessary overtime. Share data where and when necessary;

- Encourage staff input in developing unit objectives, and provide incentive for the best objective(s). Also seek staff input for improving productivity and/or reducing cost

- Provide staff with prompt feedback regarding any ideas submitted by them and discuss the ideas in staff meetings.

In summary, as a tool of financial reporting, budgets enable users to:

- Compare outcomes with actual budget figures.

- Evaluate financial performance, and thus managerial efficiency and effectiveness.

- Evaluate resource utilization as a basis for future planning and resource allocation; for example, personnel cost overruns resulting from excessive use of unbudgeted staff may indicate poor planning, especially when such extra cost cannot be tied to any volume increase or addition of new services.

- Assess adherence to generally accepted accounting principles and other regulatory mandates.

- Identify areas of cooperation through cross-functional analysis, and thus reduce or eliminate waste due to duplicate efforts.

In closing, the ideas contained in this book are not exhaustive in themselves, but merely an attempt to sensitize you to some of the things that can be of help as you make the transition from staff nurse to manager.

GLOSSARY

BOUNDED RATIONALITY   A situation whereby decision-making effectiveness is limited by time constraint, incomplete or imperfect information, complexity of the decision itself, influence of overriding variables, and variability in participant perceptions as to the consequences of the decision.

BSN   Bachelor of Science in Nursing

CLASSICAL APPROACH   The classical approach is primarily concerned with the application of systematic management and bureaucratic control toward improving efficiency in internal operations. It consists of two distinct perspectives—*scientific   management   and   administrative management.*

COST: All expenses involved in doing business; this may be money, time, material, human resource, etc. Cost may also be *fixed,* i.e. must be paid or incurred regardless of the volume of services or operation, e.g. rent; *variable,* i.e. affected by level or volume of activity, e.g. overtime pay; *direct,* i.e. easily identified with a specific department, unit, service, or activity, e.g. unit-specific supplies or equipment; and *indirect,* i.e. less obvious than direct cost, hence not easily identifiable within a unit, and may be allocated through some factor-based method such as occupancy or usage rate. Some costs may also be *controllable,* i.e. managers, supervisors or unit heads are responsible for controlling such costs, e.g. overtime, and proper use of supplies; or *non-controllable,* i.e. cannot be directly affected by the manager or supervisor; such costs are usually institutionally allocated to operating units based on some predetermined factors such as space occupied and transfer service provided.

DEPRECIATION   The systematic depletion in value and cost of a tangible asset over its estimated useful life.

DIRECT NURSING CARE: Those nursing care functions that require direct contact or observation of the patient like giving medications, starting IVs, checking vital signs, teaching patient, dressing wounds etc.

FTE (FULL TIME EQUIVALENT):   Represents the work done by someone forty hours per week, fifty-two weeks a year; 1 FTE = 2,080 hours per year (40 hours/week x 52 weeks).

INDIRECT NURSING CARE: Those functions that support nursing care, but do not require direct contact or observation of the patient, like related communication with other departments, counting narcotics, etc

MOSAIC COMPLEX A perceived sense of self-inadequacy.
PATIENT ACUITY: A measure of the severity of a patient's illness which will help the manager to more effectively determine resources necessary to deliver standard care.

PRODUCTIVITY: An expression of how designated resources are utilized to attain objectives in terms of quantity and quality. In its simplified form, productivity is expressed as the relationship of output to input, i.e. Output/Input.

TOTAL HOURS WORKED: Total amount of hours available to work minus benefit hours (vacation, sick time, and holidays).

TOTAL PAID HOURS: Total amount of hours paid to any given employee, to include benefit hours such as vacation, sick time, and holidays.

NOTES

1. Healthweek, Vol.2, No.9, p.20, May 5, 1997, Greater Dallas/Fort Worth Edition

2. Mosley, Donald C., Pietri, Paul H. & Megginson, Leon C.: Management: *Leadership In Action; 5th edition* (New York: HarperCollins College Publishers), 1996, p.584

3. Soffer, Cyril Organizations In Theory and Practice (New York: BasicBooks, Inc.), p.318

4   Daft, Richard L. *Organizing Theory & Design, 5th edition,* West Publishing Company, St. Paul, Minneapolis, p. 490, 1995.

5. Needles, Belverd E., Jr. et a. (2005). *Principles of Accounting,* Houghton Mifflin Company, pp.15, 214.

REFERENCES

Bateman, Thomas S. & Snell, Scott A. (2004). *Management: The New Competitive Landscape, 6th edition, Irwin/McGrawHill, p.30.*

Bennis, Warren & Nannus, Burt (1985). *Leaders: The Strategies for Taking Charge. Harper & Row, New York, p.22.*

Blanchard, K. et al. (1996). *Exploring the World of Business,* Worth Publishers, p. 102.

Carroll, Archie B. (1987). *In Search of the Moral Manager,* Business Horizons, p.12

Case, Bell (1997). *Career Planning for Nurses,* Delmar Publishers, New York.

Catalano, Joseph T. (1994). *Ethical And Legal Aspects of Nursing, 2nd edition,* Springhouse Corporation, Pennsylvania.

Covey, Steven *(1990):* The 7 Habits of Highly Effective People: Powerful Lessons in Personal Change,*published by Simon & Schuster (Fireside Books),New York,* p.151.

Daft, Richard L. (1995). *Organization Theory & Design, 5th edition,* West Publishing Company, St. Paul, Minneapolis, p. 490 Finkler, Steven A. (1992). *Budgeting Concepts for Nurse*

Managers, 2nd edition, W.B. Saunders Company, Philadelphia, PA 19106.

Garner, John W. (1990). *On Leadership. Free Press, New York, p.4.*

Gordon, George J. (1986). *Public Administration in America, 3rd edition,* St. Martin's Press, New York,

Green, Kenneth C. et al. (1991). *Who's Going To Run General Motors: What College Students Need to Learn Today to Become the Business Leaders of Tomorrow,* Peterson's Guides, Princeton, New Jersey.

Griffin, Ricky W. (1997). *Fundamentals of Management: Core Concepts and Applications,* Houghton Mifflin Company, Boston, *p.18*

Healthweek, Vol 2, No.9, May 5, 1997, Greater Dallas/Fort Worth Edition, p.20 Horn, Jack (1986). *Supervisor's Factomatic,* Prentice Hall, Inc., New Jersey

House, Robert J. & Mitchell, Terrence (1974). *Path Goal Theory of Leadership. Journal of Contemporary Business, Autumn, pp. 81-91.*

Ivancevich, John M. et al. (1997). *Management: Quality and Competitiveness, 2nd edition,* Richard D. Irwin, Inc., p.38.

Kindler, Herbert S. (1990). *Risk Taking: A Guide for Decision Makers,* Crisp Publications, Los Altos, CA

Langford, Teddy L. (1981). *Managing and Being Managed: A Preparation for Professional Nursing Practice,* Prentice Hall, Inc., Englewood Cliffs, NJ 07632.

Larry, Ludewig (1988). *The Ten Commandments Of Leadership, NASPA (National Association of Student Public Administrators) Journal.*

Lehan, Edward A. (1984). *Budget Making: A Workbook of Public Budgeting (Theory and Practice),* St. Martin's Press.

Mosley, Donald C. et al. (1996). *Management: Leadership In Action,* 5th *edition,* HarperCollins College Publishers, New York, p.584

Needles, Belverd E., Jr. et al. (2005). *Principles of Accounting,* Houghton Mifflin Company, pp.15, 214.

Neeley, L. Padden, et al. (1991). *Accounting: Principles and Practices,* Module 2, 4th *edition,* South-Western Publishing Company, Cincinnati.

Nickels, William G. et al. (2002). *Understanding Business,* 6th *edition,* McGraw-Hill Irwin, p.234.

Osuagwu, Christie (2004). *Nurses need to make business their business.* NurseWeek, May 3, 2004, Vol.II, No.10, p.3.

Peters, Thomas J. & Waterman, Robert H. Jr. (1982). *In Search of Excellence: Lessons from America's Best Run Companies, Warner Books, pp.13-14.*

Petzinger, Thomas (1997). *Forget Empowerment: This Job Requires Constant Brain Power. (Article in Wall Street Journal, October 17, 1997).*

Seitz, Neil (1981). *Finance for Non-financial Managers,* Reston (Prentice Hall) Publishing Company.

Sikula, Andrew, Sr. (1996). *Applied Management Ethics,* Richard D. Irwin., Inc.

Soffer, Cyril. *Organizations In Theory and Practice,* BasicBooks, Inc., New York, p.318

Uustal, Diann B. (1985). *Values and Ethics in Nursing: From Theory to Practice,* Educational Resources in Nursing and Holistic Health, p.174

Warren, Rick (2004). *The Purpose Driven Life",* Zondervan, pp.257-258, 260.

ABOUT THE AUTHORS

CHRISTIANA (CHRISTIE) C. OSUAGWU

Mrs. Christiana (Christie) C. Osuagwu is currently Director, Community Outreach and Health Disparities at the University of Texas Health Center at Tyler where she has worked for over twenty years, eighteen of which have been in different administrative management positions. She is a member of Sigma Theta Tau International Honors Society of Nursing, Texas Nurse Practitioners, and East Texas Nurse Practitioners Association. Her current role involves numerous community/public health initiatives.

Christie holds a Bachelor of Science degree in Nursing, a Master of Science degree in Public Planning and Administration – both from the University of Texas at Tyler – and a Master of Science degree in Nursing from Texas Tech University, Lubbock, Texas. She is certified as a Family Nurse Practitioner by the American Academy of Nurse Practitioners.

Her articles have appeared in professional magazines and journals such as *Advance for Nurses, the Journal of Emergency Nursing,* and *Nurse Week*

GODWIN U. OSUAGWU

Godwin U. Osuagwu holds BS and MBA degrees from Texas College and the University of Texas at Tyler, respectively.

He is currently Assistant Professor of Business at Texas College where he has taught for over nineteen years. He has also taught business as adjunct faculty in area institutions of higher learning. He was formerly a licensed nursing home administrator, and an administrator of a home health agency.

His writings include Public Corporations and the Bureaucratic Problem; The Transition of Power and Political Stability: The African Experience; a colloquium presentation on The Impact of Westernization on some Institutions in West Africa: A socio-political analysis and a case study co-authored with Dr. Mark Kroll of the University of Texas at Tyler.

Made in the USA
Middletown, DE
03 September 2021